Princess Elizabeth arrives as a prisoner
In 1550, at the age of sixteen, Princess Elizabeth was imprisoned in the Tower by her half-sister, Queen Mary. Mary was afraid that if Elizabeth were free, people would try to make her Queen. After ten weeks Elizabeth was moved to Woodstock and later Hatfield, where she was kept prisoner until Queen Mary died in 1558. Elizabeth then returned to the Tower, this time as Queen.

Site 2. Wakefield Tower

A bridge joins St Thomas's Tower to the **Wakefield Tower.** This tower guarded the main river gate in the Bloody Tower before Edward I built St Thomas's Tower. The Wakefield Tower was often called the Hall Tower, because it was attached to the Great Hall. Both were built by Henry III as parts of the royal palace. You can just see the spiral staircase which led up to the hall, on the right as you go into the Wakefield Tower.

The first room you see downstairs is the guard-room where the King's guards probably ate and rested. The room above was connected to the Great Hall and was used by the King as a private room.

It was in the Wakefield Tower that the unfortunate King Henry VI spent much of his time when he was imprisoned during the Wars of the Roses. He was a religious man, who prayed a good deal, and in the eastern recess you can see the oratory he probably used. Look for the marble tablet on the floor which reads 'By tradition Henry VI died here on May 21st, 1471'. He is supposed to have been killed that night, while at his prayers. His death is commemorated every year when on 21 May flowers are placed here – white lilies from Eton and white roses from King's College, Cambridge. Both the school and the college were founded by Henry VI.

The Wakefield Tower has also been used to store royal documents and, until moved to the new Jewel House, the Crown Jewels were on view here to the public.

Site 3. Bloody Tower

Next to the Wakefield Tower is a square building which was once called the Garden Tower. Its more terrible name was earned a long time after the death of the two young princes, Richard and Edward: the **Bloody Tower.**

The gateway was built by Henry III and the tower over it added later. Look at the huge portcullis, which weighs two tons and was raised and lowered by a system of pulleys and a capstan. Look, too, at the spikes on each side of the gateway. These are thought to have been put there on the orders of the Duke of Wellington to stop the sentries resting against the wall when on duty.

While Princess Elizabeth was imprisoned in the Lieutenant's Lodgings near the Bell Tower, three leading Protestant churchmen were arrested on the orders of her Roman Catholic half-sister, Queen Mary. Thomas Cranmer, Henry VIII's Archbishop of Canterbury, Hugh Latimer, Bishop of Worcester, and Nicholas Ridley, Bishop of London, were all imprisoned in the Bloody Tower. They were not executed here, but were taken to Oxford and burnt as heretics.

Sir Walter Raleigh was one of the most famous prisoners kept in the Bloody Tower. He was sent there for a short time by Queen Elizabeth, and then again by James I, for being involved in a plot to depose the King.

Archbishop Laud saying his last prayers, in the Bloody Tower, on the morning of his execution.

Raleigh was over fifty when he entered the Tower for the second time. He was confined to the Bloody Tower but was sometimes allowed to walk to the Lieutenant's House to dine with him. His wife and young son Wat, aged twelve, were allowed to stay with him.

He remained in the Tower for thirteen years. He started writing *The History of the World,* received visitors and even made friends with Henry, Prince of Wales, who was the same age as his own son. Some of the Lieutenants were not so friendly, and one made Raleigh's wife move to lodgings outside the Tower walls.

See if you can work out the names of six famous prisoners kept in the Bloody Tower from these anagrams:

1. HAGRIEL	**2. NRMAREC**
3. SYFJEFRE	**4. RLMAIET**
5. YDEIRL	**6. RPYCE**

Site 1. Traitors' Gate

Today you can buy a ticket which lets you into the Tower of London, but in the days when the monarchs of England lived here it was not so easy to get in, and if you were a prisoner, it was even harder to get out.

William the Conqueror and his successor, William II, built the **White Tower,** and later kings added new buildings and new defences. We call them all the Tower of London, but really over twenty towers were built. Not all of them still stand. By the time you give your ticket to the Yeoman Warder you have already passed the spot where the **Lion Tower** once stood. The royal animals, including lions and tigers, were kept in this tower.

You then walk through the **Middle Tower**, over a moat once filled with water, and through the **Byward Tower** gateway, before you have got through even the first wall defence.

By the time you can see the **Bell Tower** on

The Tower today.

The Tower in the nineteenth cent…

your left, you are inside the outer wall and looking at the solid stones which kept many famous people imprisoned. Behind the narrow arrow slits of the Bell Tower is the dark cell where Sir Thomas More spent more than a year, after he had refused to acknowledge King Henry VIII as head of the Church. At first he was allowed neither books nor pen and paper, but he managed to write to his daughter Margaret with a piece of charcoal. He was fifty-six years old, often cold, ill and in pain. When he finally knelt to be beheaded on Tower Hill in 1535 he arranged his long grey beard carefully, saying: 'Pity that were cut, for it hath committed no treason.' His head was stuck on London Bridge for six days until his daughter Margaret had it taken down.

When the King and Queen resided at the Tower of London, they often travelled here by boat. The roads were very bumpy, and boats were more comfortable than carriages. The water route was also safer for bringing important prisoners here, which is how the Water Gate got the name **Traitors' Gate.**

In the thirteenth century, King Edward I set about improving the defences of the Tower by building a new outer wall; he also built **St Thomas's Tower** to protect the approach by water. Under St Thomas's Tower is the huge arch of Traitors' Gate. It is sixty feet wide – three double-decked buses could pass through it side by side. At high tide the water came to the foot of the steps and many prisoners were brought by barge from Westminster Hall after they had been condemned to imprisonment in the Tower.

Implements of Punishment

The prisoner placed his head on the block so as to expose his neck to the executioner's axe.

To get information about plots and fellow-conspirators, or a confession of guilt, the prisoners were tortured. The rack stretched the body very painfully.

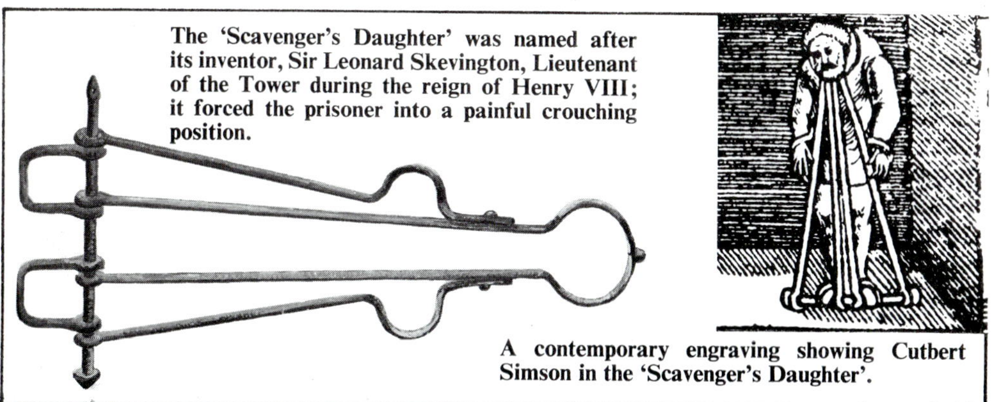

The 'Scavenger's Daughter' was named after its inventor, Sir Leonard Skevington, Lieutenant of the Tower during the reign of Henry VIII; it forced the prisoner into a painful crouching position.

A contemporary engraving showing Cutbert Simson in the 'Scavenger's Daughter'.

Sir Walter Raleigh

While a prisoner in the Tower, Sir Walter Raleigh wrote *The History of the World*. For his chemical experiments, he was allowed to use a shed in the Tower grounds and many famous scientists came to visit him. He was released by the King for an expedition to Venezuela in 1616 but after its failure was re-imprisoned and sentenced to death.

Stamp no. 17

THE HISTORY OF THE WORLD, IN FIVE BOOKS.

James I badly needed money and in 1616 he released Raleigh and sent him to Venezuela in search of treasure. When he failed to bring back any gold, the King ordered that Raleigh's former sentence for treason should be carried out, and he was executed at the Gatehouse in Westminster. He had dressed very carefully, wearing extra warm clothes so that he should not be seen to shiver, in case the crowd thought he was afraid.

In 1641 Thomas Wentworth, Earl of Strafford, passed the Bloody Tower on his way to his execution on Tower Hill. As he looked up at the window above he saw the face of his friend Archbishop Laud, who did not speak but raised his hand in blessing. Four years later Laud himself left the Bloody Tower and walked to Tower Hill. As the axe was about to cut off his head he cried out, 'I am coming, O Lord, as fast as I can.'

Make a working model of a portcullis

Materials: A sheet of card (mounting board from an art shop is best). Balsa wood (2mm square; 7mm wide × 5mm deep) and balsa 'dowel' (10mm in diameter). Cotton. Sandpaper. Glue (Uhu recommended). Modelling knife.

Construction: Draw on to the card all the sections shown below, and then cut them out. Then stick all the 7mm × 5mm balsa supports in place. Construct the gate by sticking the 2mm-square balsa horizontal bars on one side of the card frame, and the sharpened vertical bars on the other side (use the sandpaper to do this).

Construct the tower (sticking it to a base as you proceed), leaving the north side until after the gate is rigged. Cut the holes for the 'dowel', making them exactly the same size as the rod so as to achieve a good fit – you will be able to work the rod through the card. Rig up the gate with cotton as shown, and stick the end of the cotton around the rod with glue.

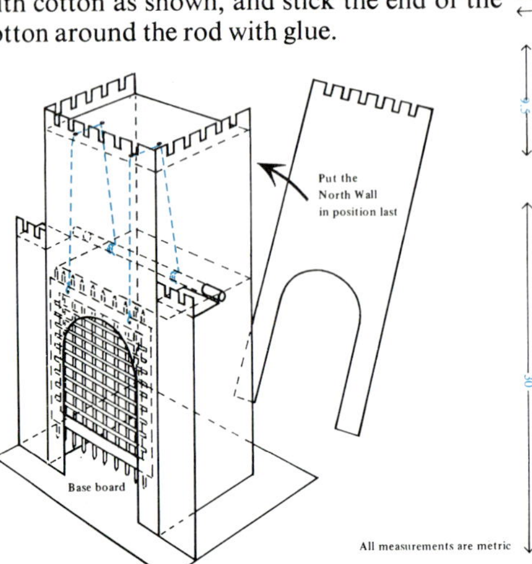

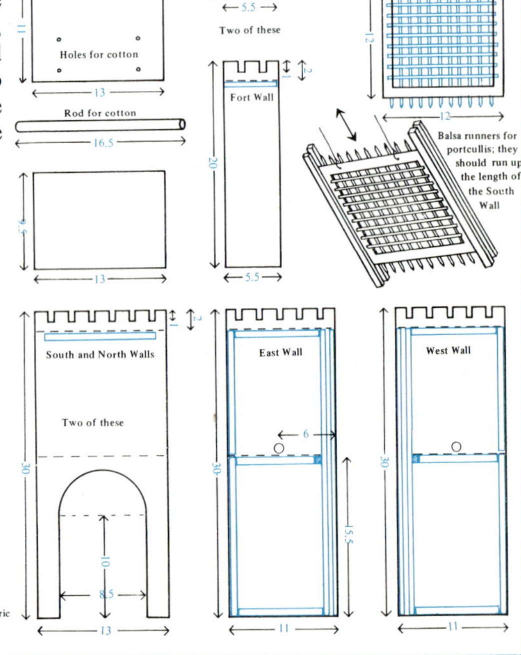

What happened to the Princes?

When Edward IV died in 1483, the crown went to his twelve-year-old son Edward. With his uncle, Richard, Duke of Gloucester, he entered the Tower to await his coronation.

A child-king needs an adult to help him rule, and Gloucester now became young Edward's Protector. He persuaded the King's mother, Elizabeth Woodville, to let her other son, Richard, join his brother for company. Then, with both boys safely confined (in the Bloody Tower), Gloucester had himself crowned as Richard III. The children were seldom seen, and eventually their deaths were announced.

This is one of the Tower's mysteries. The usual story is that their uncle organised their murder. Assassins entered their room as they slept and suffocated them, 'keping down by force the fetherbed and pillowes hard unto their mouthes'.

But supposing they were not dead, but only prisoners? Two years later Richard III was slain, and Henry VII ruled England. Those children, if they were still alive, had a better right to the throne than he did. So another possibility is that they were murdered on *his* orders.

Time-table of events

1483	**April 9**	Death of Edward IV. Young king in care of the Woodvilles, his mother's relatives.
	April 30	Woodvilles arrested by Gloucester and accused of plot to seize power. Elizabeth Woodville takes sanctuary at Westminster, with younger son and daughters.
	May	Gloucester made Protector by the Council.
	June 16	Richard, Duke of York, joins Edward V in the Tower.
	June 25	Gloucester, urged by Parliament, takes the crown.
	July 6	Gloucester crowned Richard III.
1484	**January**	Chancellor of France, in a speech, accuses Richard III of child-murder.
1485	**August**	Battle of Bosworth. Richard III killed. Henry VII becomes king.
1491		Rebellion of Perkin Warbeck, claiming to be Richard, Duke of York.
1502		Sir James Tyrell confesses to the murder of the Princes, in summer 1483.
1646		Sir George Buck writes a history book, and says Edward V died naturally and Richard, Duke of York, escaped to France.
1674		Workmen discover bones against the wall of the White Tower.
1678		Bones interred in Westminster Abbey.
1933		Bones examined by royal commission and declared to be those of two children, roughly the age of the Princes.

Sites 4 and 5. Queen's House and Scaffold Site

The night before her execution Anne Boleyn was kept awake by the noise of sawing and hammering. The scaffold was being built. It was a square wooden platform draped in black. Anne Boleyn dressed herself in a robe of grey damask with a white ermine collar, and at noon she climbed up to the scaffold. It was the custom to pay the executioner and she handed him a purse with £20 in it. He had already received £23 6s. 8d. for a new suit of black clothes for the occasion. She spoke a few words to the small group of people, saying that she died willingly, condemned by the law of the land and reproaching no one. She knelt to pray, her eyes were bandaged, and the executioner cut off her head with one stroke of the sword.

Several famous prisoners were executed on Tower Green; among them were two Queens, Katherine Howard and Lady Jane Grey. They were all fortunate in having very few people to watch.

Other important people were usually executed on Tower Hill, outside the walls of the Tower, and ordinary criminals were hanged at Tyburn – where Marble Arch now stands. Crowds flocked to watch, as they do now for a football match or a pop concert. The picture on the inside front cover shows you the crowds that came to the execution of Lord Lovat.

The bodies of the people executed on Tower Green were buried in the chapel of St Peter ad Vincula, which you can see beyond the railings.

With your back to the chapel, you are looking at the **Queen's House,** where the Governor now lives.

It was from this building that the Earl of Nithsdale made one of the most daring escapes in the history of the Tower. Dressed

Why Anne Boleyn was executed
When Henry VIII grew tired of his second wife, Anne Boleyn, and it was obvious that she would not give him the son he wanted, he accused her of being unfaithful. She was accused and tried for treason and sentenced to be executed. She asked to be beheaded with a sword, and both sword and executioner were brought over specially from France.

The Scaffold Site on Tower Green with the royal Chapel of St Peter ad Vincula in the background.

Queen's House which stands on the south side of Tower Green.

as a woman, he walked out of the Tower followed by his devoted wife, who had planned the disguise, and they fled to Italy.

Also facing Tower Green is the house of the Yeoman Gaoler, which stands on the site of the house where Lady Jane Grey lived when she was imprisoned in the Tower. She was only fifteen and had been Queen of England for nine days when she saw her husband, Guildford Dudley, leave the Beauchamp Tower for his execution on Tower Hill. A short time later she watched his headless body being brought back for burial. The next day she herself was executed on Tower Green.

The Council Chamber in Queen's House.

Site 6. Beauchamp Tower

A prisoner starts a new inscription.

The **Beauchamp Tower** was probably named after Thomas Beauchamp, third Earl of Warwick, who was a prisoner here in the fourteenth century in the reign of Richard II. Beauchamp (pronounced Beecham) was his family name.

This tower has often been used for prisoners of high rank, and it has some interesting inscriptions on its walls. Some of them were carved in these rooms, others have been brought here from other parts of the Tower.

Prisoners scratched on the walls with anything they could find: a nail, a pin, a broken knife. Sometimes they wrote their name, carved their family crest or wrote of their faith.

Before the Spanish Armada, the Tower was full of priests and Roman Catholic noblemen imprisoned by Queen Elizabeth for plotting against the Protestants. Elizabeth was anxious to crush any support for the Roman Catholic King of Spain. One of these noblemen was Philip, Earl of Arundel. During his time in prison he carved the Latin words over the fireplace. See if you can make them out. QUANTO PLUS AFFLICTIONIS PRO CHRISTO IN HOC SAECULO, TANTO PLUS GLORIAE CUM CHRISTO IN FUTURO, ARUNDELL, 22 JUNE 1587. That means: 'The greater the misery we endure for Christ in this world, the more glory shall we have with Him in the next.' Arundel died a natural death in the Tower in 1595.

The name JANE appears twice (numbers 48 and 85), probably carved not by Lady Jane Grey but by her husband, Lord Guildford Dudley, or his brother. The Dudley brothers carved the elaborate family crest pictured on the opposite page.

Scotland

Wales

England

Ireland

United Kingdom

Find the stamps for these squares and stick them in.

All the Queen's Beasts are shown on this magnificent vase. Also on the vase are the symbols of the different regions of the United Kingdom: a rose for England, a leek for Wales, a thistle for Scotland, a shamrock for Ireland, and a lion and a unicorn for the whole United Kingdom.

Thomas Abell, chaplain to Queen Katherine of Aragon. He has carved the letter A on to a bell to make his name.

The Dudley Brothers, 1553. A bear and a lion are holding a ragged staff and flowers representing four of the brothers' names surround the crest.

Make your own 'wall' inscription

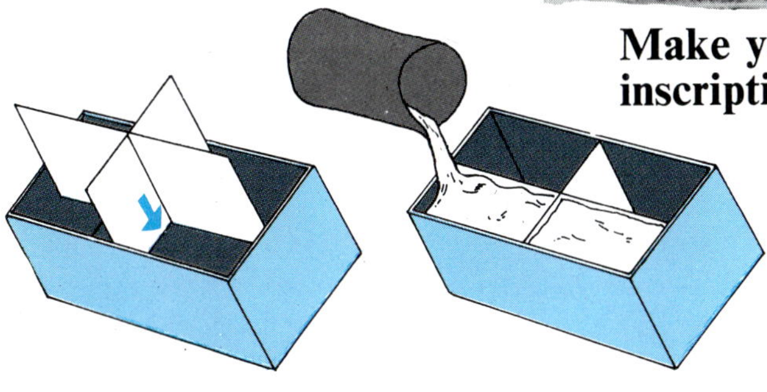

Split a shoe box into four equal sections by placing cardboard 'walls' across the box. Mix up enough plaster-of-paris to fill the box. Allow it to dry. You and your friends can then carve your name or initials, using a suitable instrument. Colour with grey paint to achieve the final 'realistic' look.

Site 7. White Tower

William the Conqueror began this great stone keep, and his son, William Rufus, finished it. A Norman, named Gundulf, supervised the building of the Tower. He later became Bishop of Rochester. The White Tower looks square. In fact its west side is 107 feet, its south side 118 feet. Only one corner is a right angle. The walls vary from 11 to 15 feet thick and rise to 90 feet high. They were often whitewashed, and Henry III ordered lead gutters to carry rainwater from the roof, so as not to spoil their appearance.

The White Tower, as well as being a castle and the seat of government, was the home of the medieval kings until Henry III built a palace on its south side. Then it became a residence for guests, or prisoners, among them Charles of Orleans. He was confined there for twenty-five years after the Battle of Agincourt.

1. North-east turret, used in 1675 as the Royal Observatory.
2. Council Chamber. Here, in 1399, Richard II was forced to give up his throne.
3. Banqueting hall, used for celebrations.
4. Guard room, where soldiers on duty waited. Some weapons were kept here.
5. Basement, for stores of food and arms, with a well 40 feet deep.
6. The stairways have a right-hand spiral. This left the sword-arm free for action.
7. Entrance at first-floor level, out of reach of a battering-ram.
8. Wall passages led to private apartments. The royal family lived here until the palace was built in the thirteenth century.
9. Chapel of St John, one of England's finest pieces of Norman architecture.

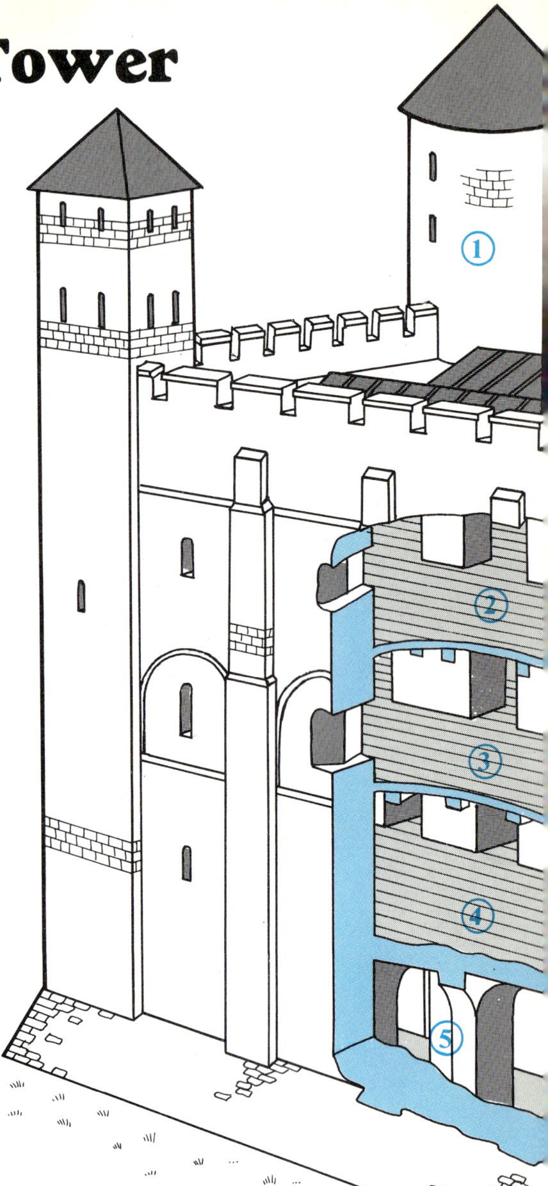

A cut-away drawing of the White Tower. With the exception of an additional floor on top level (2), added at a later stage, and the stone vaults built in the eighteenth century, this is how the keep would have looked at the time of William II (c. 1100).

Stamp no. 24

Stamp no. 25

Before mass-production, weapons were precious. They were closely guarded in the armouries.

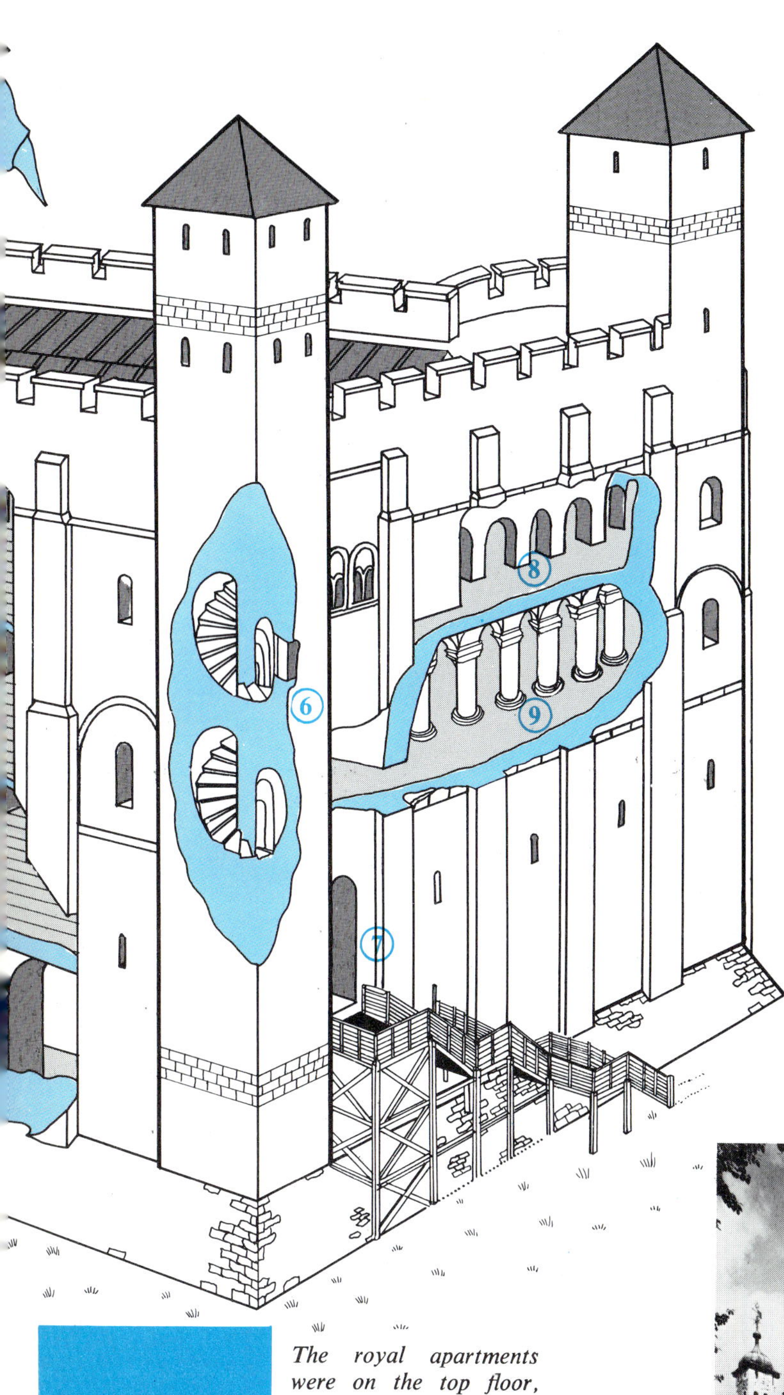

Stamp no. 26

The royal apartments were on the top floor, reached by staircases in the corner towers and by wall passages. They were made comfortable, with fireplaces and latrines in the wall-thicknesses.

Stamp no. 27

In the Middle Ages there was no Parliament as we know it today. The King took advice from his Great Council. Orders passed by the Council were sent all through the land.

Stamp no. 28

Table manners were not like ours. Knives and spoons were used, but no forks. Joints of meat were roasted on spits.

Stamp no. 29

Sporting and Tournament Galleries

Inside the White Tower is a museum of arms and armour. There has been a museum here since the days of Henry VIII and it is one of the oldest in Europe.

As you walk in you might almost be in a European hunting castle with the trophies of the hunt on the walls. Noblemen spent a great deal of time hunting duck, deer, boar and other wild game. You can see guns and crossbows of the kind that were used.

When the nobles weren't hunting or fighting real battles they fought mock battles to keep in practice and to entertain themselves and their friends. Mock battles took the form of jousts or tournaments. A joust was a fight between two knights on horseback, whereas a tournament was a fight between two groups of knights.

Foot tournaments were also fought, sometimes with a barrier between the opponents, so that there was no need to wear leg armour. The aim was to get the better of the other fighter either by hitting him an agreed number of times or by knocking him over.

An animal frieze taken from the stock of a German wheel-lock gun of about 1660. This hunting scene is inlaid in stag horn and mother-of-pearl.

Chapel of St John

You can usually tell the age of a church by the shape of its arches. Norman arches are usually round, and the Chapel of St John is the oldest Norman church in London and one of the most beautiful in England. The building of the Chapel was completed during or shortly after the reign of William the Conqueror and it has always been used as a private royal chapel.

Here Queen Mary Tudor was married to King Philip II of Spain. As Philip could not come to London, Count Egmont took his place as proxy at the ceremony.

The Order of the Bath

Stamp no. 30

A ceremony creating Knights of the Bath is known to have taken place at the Tower of London on at least two occasions. One was in 1399 when, on the morning of his Coronation, Henry IV created forty-six new knights and the other in 1461 when the new King Edward IV created twenty-seven. On the eve of the ceremony, those to be knighted probably kept vigil in the Chapel of St John. After the ceremony, they rode in procession with the King to his Coronation.

Medieval Gallery

In the room next to the Chapel of St John, you can see arms and armour ranging from the earliest in the Tower collection up to the end of the fifteenth century.

In front of you as you enter is a mail shirt. You can see the metal rings which protected the body of the knight. As you walk through the gallery you will see how pieces of plate were gradually added to the body to give even more protection from swords and arrows; by the time you get to the other end you will see that the armourers have learnt how to make plate-armour which can move easily with the man and the horse. You will see too that the best armour was made mainly in Italy and Germany.

While knights were covering themselves in stronger armour, the first firearms were being made. Look for the book that explains how to make gun-powder, and look too for the very early cannon in the case with the mail shirt.

In the last case before the next gallery there is a cross-bow. The English used this bow mainly for sport. It took longer to make ready for shooting than the long-bow, which was the great English fighting weapon.

Stamp no. 31

Some swords are used for cutting an enemy, some for thrusting at him. This huge sword was used for neither. It is a bearing sword which was carried upright in processions.

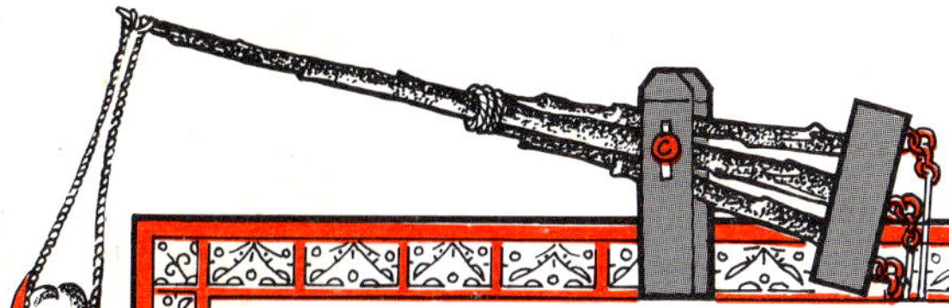

The History of Arms & Armour
(13th–17th Centuries)

When you turn this page you will find a special section, showing the different kinds of armour and weapons that men made and used over a period of five hundred years.

Man's first weapon was probably a stick. When he learnt how to use metal, the stick gave way to a sword. Then soldiers began to wear some sort of helmet and to carry a shield on one arm. By Norman times, when the Tower of London was begun, men were well protected in battle. Every century after that saw more improvements, right up to the time of the Civil War (1642–52).

In the Middle Ages, the longbow was one of the best weapons. At a siege, catapults like the one at the top of this page hurled great stones at enemy armies and castles. Gunpowder changed this, slowly. Hand guns and cannon were easier to use and faster to reload and fire.

Thirteenth Century **Fourteenth Century**

Thirteenth Century
The Norman soldier wore a *hauberk,* a shirt of mail made from thousands of little iron rings, interlaced and riveted together. He also wore a sword and carried an axe. His shoes were made of oiled leather and, to protect his head, he wore an iron *chapel-de-fer* or *kettle-hat*. The mounted soldier, in the background of the picture, wears a flat-topped *helm* and carries a lance and small shield. His horse has a cloth cover called a *trapper* or *caparison*.

Fourteenth Century
In the picture you can see the Black Prince who died in 1376. Mail soon gave way to plate-armour, which was heavy to wear and difficult to move about in. A mail collar, the *aventail,* protected the neck. The bowman behind him wears a quilted canvas tunic over a mail shirt and an iron helmet. Notice the *bracer* on

PRICE 25 MILS.

A BRIEF HISTORY AND DESCRIPTION OF KYRENIA CASTLE

KYRENIA CASTLE

HISTORY. A Greek inscription of the Flavian era found in the castle, in which people of "Kyrenes" honoured a benefactor, indicates that the medieval town was built on the site of the ancient. The latter, whose name seems to connect it with the Achaean colonists, was an independent city with its king until it was absorbed by Salamis in 312 B.C. Four years previously Seleucus had taken it by siege, indicating the city was already walled. Of the Roman period some tombs survive and the breakwater protecting the castle. A bishopric from the time of Constantine, Kyrenia preserves relics of its early churches in the marble columns used as bollards in the harbour and others with capitals re-used in the Byzantine chapel in the castle, which probably occupies the site of the acropolis of the ancient city.

It is more than likely that the castle existed and the town was walled at the time of the first Arab raids in the mid-seventh century. It was doubtless the survival of the town walls of that period which made it necessary for Kyrenia to be taken by assault by the Byzantine force sent to quell a rebellion in A.D. 1092, while the position of the twelfth century Byzantine chapel is such that the castle must antedate it.

To this Early Byzantine Castle of Kyrenia Isaac Comnenus sent his wife, daughter and treasures during Richard Lionheart's campaign in 1191. After the battle at Tremethousha Richard, who fell ill at Nicosia, charged Guy de Lusignan with the task of reducing Kyrenia, which surrendered after a brief attack.

That the castle was already important in the early years of the Lusignan kingdom is clear from the role it played in the struggle between the Imperialists and the Royalists (1228—1233), when it frequently changed hands. In 1228 the Emperor Frederick II on his way to the Holy Land was prompted by his partisans in Cyprus to land and demand the revenues of the kingdom during the minority of the young king Henry I. Kyrenia and the other castles were occupied by the adherents of the young king and his champion John D' Ibelin, Lord of Beirut, who had assumed the regency on the death of his brother Philip, whom the High Court had appointed. A clash was inevitable, but at first a truce was arranged, during which both parties joined Frederick's crusading expedition. Meanwhile the emperor's supporters gained control in the Island and the next year when Ibelin returned to Cyprus he found them in possession of the castles and the young king in their hands. Ibelin, after worsting them in an engagement near Nicosia, besieged the castles to which they fled. Kyrenia surrendered on terms and the other later capitulated.

The castle changed hands again in 1232 when Ibelin withdrew his forces to protect his possessions at Beirut, against which the emperor on returning to Italy had sent a new force of Longobard troops. The emperor's Cypriot supporters took the opportunity to return to and overrun Cyprus, where Kyrenia at first held out, but not for long. The Longobard army followed them, having done serious mischief to Ibelin in Syria, established themselves in Famagusta and provisioned Kyrenia. Hot on their heels came Ibelin and the young King Henry with him. They ejected the Longobards from Famagusta and engaged the main body at Agirda, where they were blocking the pass to Kyrenia. The Longobards, despite their greater numbers, were out-fought and withdrew to Kyrenia, which under the command of Philip Chenart they gallantly defended. With the defenders was the young Queen Alice of Montferrat, whom the Emperor had given Henry in marriage. She can have seen little of her husband and during the siege fell sick and died. The besiegers employed mangonels and trebuchets, and two great wooden towers which were drawn over the fosse, where the king lost one of his most valiant knights, Anseau de Brie. The siege was long and costly, Genoese galleys being employed to prevent provisioning of the castle by sea, but after ten months the Longobards abandoned hope of relief by the emperor and surrendered the castle to the king in exchange for safe-conduct to Tyre.

From this time when the first Frankish additions to the Byzantine fortress may already have been made, the castle remained firmly in possession of the crown, held by a "Chief and Castellan of the Castle and the Bourg for the King". The distinction between the Castle proper and the bourg or walled town adjoining it is noteworthy, it is not always clear which is referred to in accounts of the sieges. The castle was drastically remodelled on some later occasion which is not recorded, probably after the loss of Acre in 1291 when the defences of the kingdom were strengthened; the north and east ranges were completely rebuilt and on the south the castle was extended by erecting, right outside its previous limits, a massive new wall. Some of these improvements may not have been completed before the late fourteenth century.

Thus strengthened, the castle commended itself for use as a state prison. Upwards of twenty of the nobles and knights who had supported Amaury's unsurpation were here confined in 1310, after his assassination and Henry II's return. The leaders were later sent to the oubliettes, "very dark and horrible", the Prince of Galilee by himself and the others in pairs, to die a lingering death by starvation.

More commodious evidently was the cell of Aimery de Minars who in 1343 employed his imprisonment in the castle on transcribing the *Gestes des Chiprois*, and happily so, for his is the only copy that has survived. Here Hugh IV in 1349 imprisoned his two sons as punishment for their abortive attempt to pay a clandestine visit to Europe. One of them when he succeeded to the throne as Peter I must therefore have found special satisfaction in committing his enemies to the cells, among them the ambassadors sent by the Mameluke Sultan in 1368. They were followed, during Peter's absence in Europe the same year, by his own mistress Jeanne Laleman who had been sent to the castle by Eleanor his jealous queen, and in the sad crisis which ended in his assassination the dungeons at Kyrenia were seldom empty.

In the history of the castle the climax came a few years later, when the Genoese seized Famagusta, sacked Nicosia and laid siege to Kyrenia by land and sea. The constable (later King James I) refused all demands of the Genoese for surrender of the place in the name of the young King Peter II, who was in their power. His spirited defence with arbalests, stone-throwers and Greek fire obliged the attackers to move their camp; and the garrison of St. Hilarion castle made effective sallies against their lines of communication. After failure of renewed attacks the Genoese brought round ships from Famagusta carrying siege-engines, including a mangonel which threw a very large stone. But even when these were reinforced by a fleet from Genoa they achieved nothing. Of the giant fighting towers brought up by land some were burnt or over-turned by the defenders in bold sallies and others destroyed by trebuchets operating behind the shelter of the walls. After nearly two months of fruitless efforts the Genoese withdrew and in the treaty confining their jurisidiction to Famagusta they agreed to grant the Constable safe conduct to the west. He was however intercepted at sea and imprisoned in Genoa.

The terms exacted by the Genoese for his liberation as laid down in the treaty of 1383 provided that, apart from the surrender of Famagusta, Kyrenia also to be taken over in pledge. It seems unlikely that this was ever done, for after James's return and coronation in 1385 the castle became his favourite residence. It is probable that further improvements to the castle were carried out in his reign. In 1426, when the Mamelukes overran the Island and King Janus was captured, the Regent took the royal family and treasures to Kyrenia castle for safety. The invaders withdrew without investing it.

Kyrenia was again besieged in 1460, when James the Bastard usurped the throne from his legitimate step-sister Charlotte and the latter repaired to Kyrenia with her husband Louis of Savoy and their supporters. James, employing artillery and Mameluke aid, attacked the place. A cannon mounted on a Greek church did great damage, but the fortress itself was well supplied with artillery. It was nearly four years before Charlotte's supporters were forced while she herself was in Italy, to surrender this her last foothold in the kingdom, after they had been reduced to eating dogs, cats and mice.

It was left to the Venetians to adapt the castle for artillery warfare. The west wall was entirely rebuilt and massive towers with numerous gun-emplacements were constructed on the north-west and south-east angles. The new west wall was raised in 1544, and in 1560 a great rectangular bastion was added at the south-west corner. On the eve of the Turkish conquest further improvements were being considered as the earlier Venetian additions were already absolete. In the event they were never put to the test, for the fortress was surrendered in 1570 on the first demand of the Turkish admiral, so disheartened were the garrison by the news of the fall of Nicosia.

The castle was once more invested following the revolt of its commandant Khalil Agha in 1765. Forces sent from the mainland to deal with the situation, having filled the ditch, failed to storm the walls, but an effective blocade forced the rebel to surrender. During the British occupation the castle was used first as a prison and then until 1950 as a police barracks and training school. In that year it passed to the custody of the Department of Antiquities for maintainance as an Ancient Monument. The removal of modern accretions and the repair of the ancient fabric had almost been completed when, in the Summer of 1955, it passed once more into military occupation. Until it was returned to the Department of Antiquities over four years later, it was garrisoned by units of the British security forces and used as a place of internment for members of the EOKA organisation.

DESCRIPTION. (The reference numbers in brackets in the text are marked on the corresponding parts of the castle on the plan following page 7). The castle is approached by a bridge across the west ditch and is entered by a gate, formerly furnished with a drawbridge. The high west wall in which the gate opens is Venetian throughout and was completed in 1544. There are indications that before the Venetians remodelled the castle the outer west wall was in approximately the same position. Within the gate a vaulted entrance passage of Venetian construction (1) leads up to the west ward, passing (on the right) a staircase descending to a sally-port and (on the left) the entry to a parallel passage by which the *Byzantine Chapel* is reached. Adjoining the chapel passage two Venetian guard-rooms (2) have been contrived, from one of which the entrance passage underneath could be controlled.

The Byzantine Chapel (3) is a twelfth century building with a dome (restored) carried on four marble columns, which, like their capitals, were taken from some earlier building. It is possible that an Early Byzantine basilica had previously occupied the same site. The chapel, standing outside the main part of the castle, may well have continued in use for the Greek rite under the Lusignans. Originally the chapel stood free in the outer ward of the Byzantine and Frankish castle, but the Venetians filled it round, removed the dome and used it simply as a means of access to their new north-west tower, which is still reached through its west door. The Venetian passage leading to this tower was in part constructed within a small narthex which had been added to the Byzantine Chapel in the Frankish period. Beyond the narthex the passage was cut through the Byzantine and Frankish walls that formed the limit of the west ward at its northern end.

In the interior of *Outer North-West Tower* (4) the angle of the Frankish castle can be seen. From the staircase which descends within it to the level of the ditch (into which there is a sally port) gun-chambers on several levels can be reached.

Returning to the chapel and leaving by its north door, the visitor reaches an area outside its east end, (5) where the Venetian filling, once level with the chapel roof, has been removed. This area was almost cut off from the rest of the west ward by the successive additions in the Frankish period to the inner north-west tower. What remains of the west ward is regained through a modern breach in the wall of the Venetian passage to the chapel.

The West Ward (6) was reduced by the Venetians to a small area in front of the Frankish gatehouse on the inner west wall, which to the north of the gatehouse survives in its original Byzantine form. Here starts the broad, dog-leg ramp, which carried the Venetian artillery to the ramparts, it rests in part on massive fillings of earth between the inner and outer west walls, in part on a series of casemates and vaulted chambers constructed against the latter, two of which are furnished with gunports.

The Gatehouse (7), a Frankish fourteenth century structure which possibly replaced a Byzantine original, contains the bent entrance into the main courtyard. It had only one gate, but this was reinforced with a portcullis. The coats of arms over the gate are medieval, but in this position they are a modern insertion. At the angle of the entrance passage is the tomb of Sadik Pasha of Algiers, commander of the Turkish fleet, who died in September 1570 at the time of the Turkish conquest.

Entering the *Courtyard* the massive facade of the Frankish east range is seen opposite. The north end of the Courtyard was occupied by other Frankish buildings of which only the foundations remain, with a huge basement cistern (still in use). At the southern end, which the visitor should see first, are extensive remains of the Byzantine fortress. Here and on the west side the courtyard is still enclosed by Byzantine masonry.

The West Range: Doorways cut through the section of the Byzantine west wall southward from the gatehouse lead into the chambers which were added outside the early wall under the Lusignans. In the floor of the lowest of these (8) two rock-cut shafts, opening out below the neck, are no doubt the *oubliettes* where so many distinguished prisoners languished. This lower chamber was originally also entered through an archway (reopened 1953) from the west ward, which lay between this building and the outer west wall of the castle and which, at this point, was filled by the Venetian ramp. The part of the filling carrying the ramp which lay next to the wall of the west range was cut away in 1952-53 to form a trench along the face of the wall; at the same time the ramp was supported with a retaining wall so that the door and windows of the west range could be re-opened.

The middle storey of this range, which these windows light, is reached by a staircase from the courtyard (9). It contains a large chamber of four bays of slightly-pointed, intersecting vaulting divided by transverse arches. The arches are carried on corbels of the primitive quarter-round type, suggesting that this is one of the earliest Lusignan additions, dating from the thirteenth century. The rather large windows suggest that the outer west wall of the Frankish castle must have risen to a good height to protect them, and the same time indicate the domestic character of the apartment.

Outside the door of this chamber, a staircase against the Byzantine wall, which probably once led to its battlements, now leads to what is left of the upper storey of the Frankish west range. Here, it has been suggested, were situated the royal apartments of the later Lusignans. However that may be, this upper storey is reasonably preserved only in the fourteenth-century gatehouse section, which is occupied by a small, roofless *Chapel* with large windows to west and north. This was the chapel proper of the Frankish castle, used for the Latin rite. A sacristy to the north retains its vaulted roof. The chapel was entered from the south, through a vestibule which opens through an arch onto a gallery carried on arches and corbels outside the east wall of the chapel, now lost, which was of shallow apsidal form.

The gallery provided for circulation along this level of the ınge without passing through the chapel. At its north end, rcase leads to the northern section of the west range, where

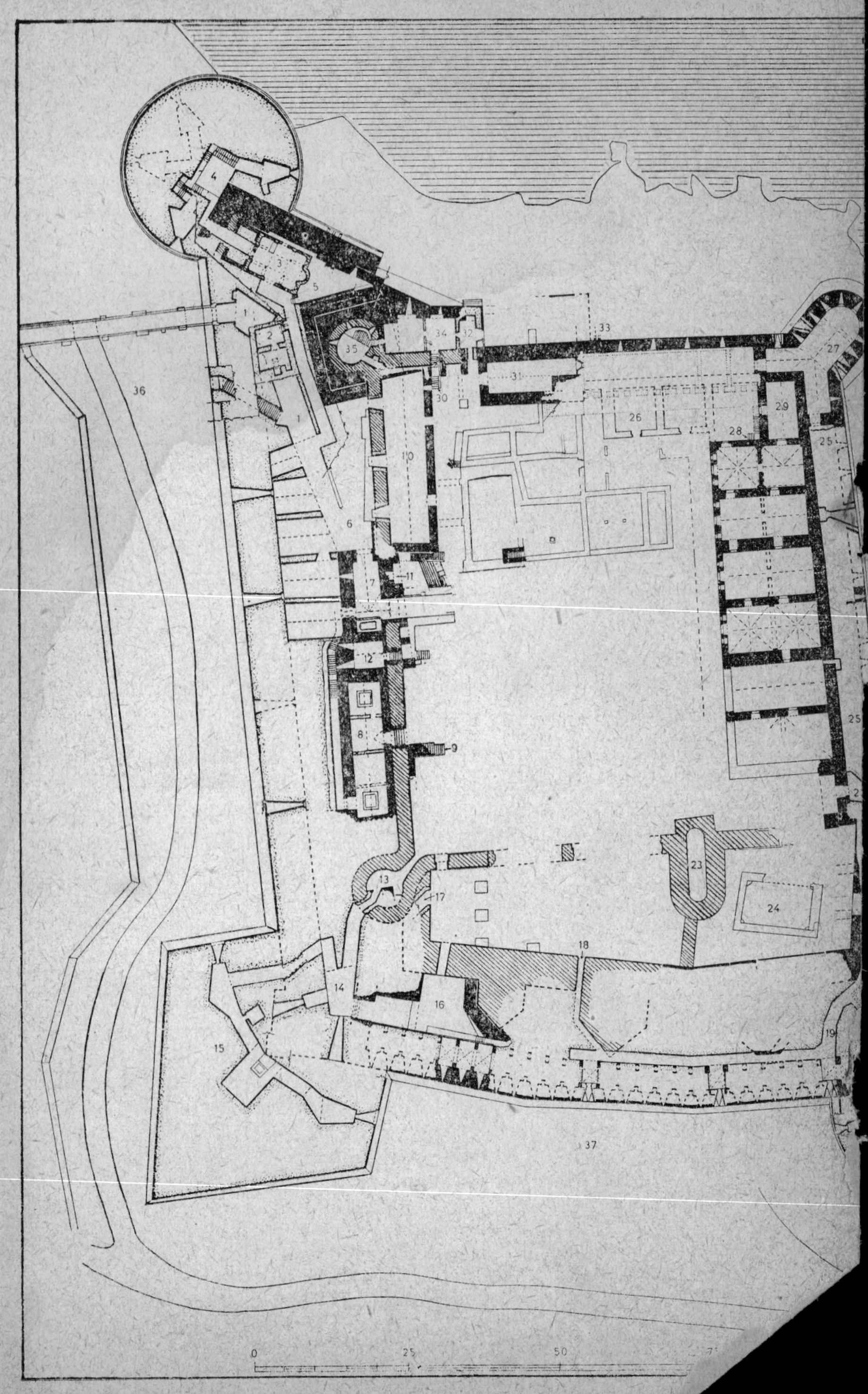
4
3
5
1
2
35
34
32
33
31
30
27
29
26
28
25
36
1
10
6
11
7
12
8
9
25
23
13
17
24
18
14
16
19
15
37
0
25
50

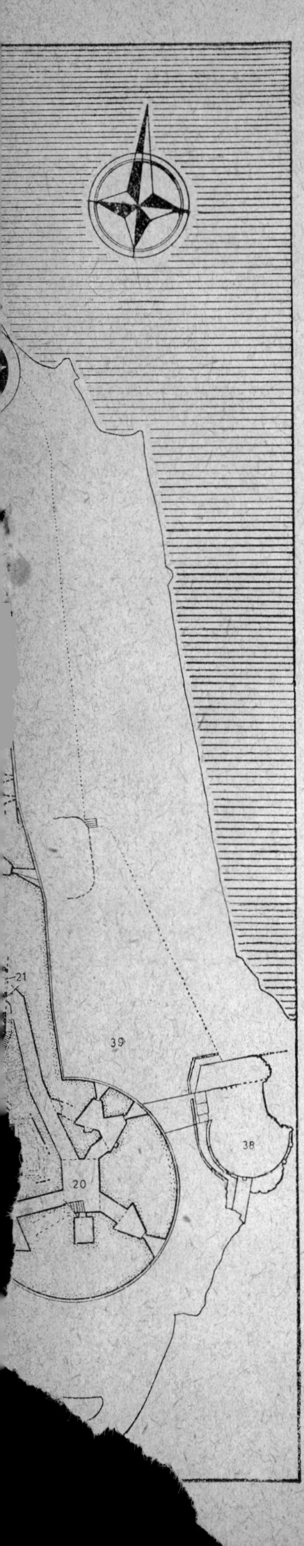

Hatched walls	=	Byzantine castle
Black walls	=	Frankish reconstructions and additions
Dotted walls	=	Venetian reconstructions and additions

1— Entrance passage.
2— Guardroom.
3— Byzantine Chapel.
4— North-West Tower.
5— West Ward (north end).
6— West Ward (centre).
7— Gate-House (chapel over).
8— Undercroft with oubliettes.
9— To West Range (upper storeys).
10— Early Frankish Undercroft.
11— To Gate-House (middle storey).
12— Vaulted cell.
13— South-West Tower (Byzantine).
14— West Ward, South End (Venetian gun-chamber).
15— South-West Bastion.
16— South Ward.
17— To South-West Bastion (lower level).
18— To South Fighting Gallery.
19— Venetian Gallery.
20.— South-East Tower.
21— Gate to East Outwork.
22— Gun-Chamber (site of Frankish tower).
23— Horseshoe Tower.
24— Water Tank.
25.— East Fighting Gallery.
26— North Range (foundations).
27— North-East Tower.
28— North-East Staircase.
29 Chamber with reconstructed floor.
30— North-West Staircase.
31— Undercroft.
32— Postern Gate.
33— Site of Frankish Postern.
34.—Forebuilding.
35— Inner North-West Tower.
36— West Ditch.
37— South Ditch.
38— Base of Tower.
39— Site of East Outwork.

only the outline of a large upper chamber added in the fourteenth century can be seen. Another staircase descends to the courtyard, which it reaches in a narrow alley between the best range and the foundations of the extensive buildings which once occupied the north end of the courtyard. The west range, on the ground level, comprises in the northern section a long and lofty undercroft (10) built against the inside of the original Byzantine west wall. This is one of the earliest Frankish structures in the castle and probably dates from the early thirteenth century.

South of it a broad flight of steps leads up to the middle level of the gatehouse (11). In this chamber, above the gate, the portcullis was operated and from it a good watch could be kept both on the west ward and on the interior of the castle. A doorway in its west wall, which is not original, leads onto the west ward ramp and into the trench cut between it and the west range in 1952.

To complete the tour of the west range the visitor should return to the courtyard and pass under the southernmost of the arches carrying the gallery. Here steps lead down to a square chamber with a high vaulted roof (12) it has two tiny windows with steeply sloping sills high in the west wall, and its entrance was formerly furnished with double doors. This chamber, which is constructed in the same high quality masonry as the rest of the gatehouse block, may well have been designed as a cell for distinguished prisoners.

At the south-west angle of the courtyard is the entry to the original corner tower at the junction of the inner south and west walls of the Byzantine castle (13). It was a circular form but part of the interior is occupied by a massive pier inserted to underpin some later structure that was built on top of it. Part of the circular external face has been disengaged in excavations at rampart level.

A breach in the wall of this tower and a passage, constructed when the Venetians filled the south end of the west ward, lead to a gun-chamber with two gun-ports at the south-west angle of the original Venetian reconstructions (14). From this angle gun-chamber a branch passage cuts through a gun-port of the west wall to reach the middle level to the great *south-west bastion* outside it (15). This bastion was added in 1560 to provide gun positions on three levels enfilading the south and west arms of the ditch. Those on its ramparts can have been reached only from the large open shaft which links the two gun-chambers on this middle level. Here the high quality of the Venetian masonry may be noted.

From the angle gun-chamber a Frankish gateway with portcullis slots leads to an area of the *South Ward* excavated in 1952-1953 (16). This is bounded on the north by the outer Byzantine south wall, on the east by one of its solid pentagonal towers encased in later Frankish masonry, and on the south by the new south wall constructed outside it in the fourteenth century. In the latter a section of the vaulted fighting gallery, which the Venetians had filled with masonry, has been reopened. This and other areas between the Frankish and the Byzantine walls, which had been left open to form an outer ward on this south side of the Frankish castle, were filled with earth by the Venetians to form a rampart over 22 meters thick. The courtyard is regained through a small postern gate in the outer Byzantine wall, flanked by two couchant lions in relief and surmounted by a third. These were probably taken from some building of the Roman period, as were the column drums of limestone used near the top of the wall.

On returning to the courtyard the visitor will find, on the left, an opening (17) which leads into another passage, sloping steeply down to the lowest level of the *South-West Bastion*. From the high central chamber on this level, the original angle of the Venetian castle can be seen above the mouth of the entrance passage. It seems likely that the walls of the pre-Venetian castle also formed a simple angle at this point, without any projecting angle tower, a most unusual arrangement. Gun-chambers open on either side of the central chamber of the bastion, as in the upper level, to provide flanking fire for the south and west arms of the ditch. A narrow passage leads to a well near the point of the bastion.

Returning to the courtyard and traversing an area with remains of vaults between the inner and outer Byzantine south walls, the entrance to a narrow passage cut through the latter is reached (18). This leads to the *Venetian South Gallery* from which gunports opened in the Frankish south wall were served.. This gallery was formed when the Venetians filled with earth the various sections of the south ward between the Frankish and the outer Byzantine south walls. Originally it was reached only by the vertical shaft at the west end, the present entrance passage passing along the flank of one of the pentagonal Byzantine towers was opened in 1950. Except for the three bays retained as gun-chambers almost the whole of the vaulted fighting gallery of the Frankish castle was walled up with masonry by the Venetians; previously it was open to the south ward. At the extreme east end the original form of the fighting-gallery with it loopholes can be seen; since it was here encased in the Venetian south-west tower it was considered superfluous to wall up this section. At this end the Venetian passage turned north (19) as though to emerge into the courtyard, but if this was the intention it was never carried out, for the passage came to a dead end. In 1957 it was extended to join the passage leading to the interior of the Venetian south-east tower from the courtyard. The modern section passes along the face of what must once have been the outside wall of the castle.

The *South-East Tower* (20), circular without, is similar to the north-west tower in having a lofty rectangular chamber from which the gun positions on different levels are reached, but here there is no staircase and no sally port. Opposite the entrance passage, which was once closed by a door, is a small powder store. The masonry, which is Venetian throughout, is in remarkably perfect condition.

The courtyard is regained near its south-east angle where the southermost vaults of the Franklish east range have fallen. These vaults were not constructed together with the east wall, against which they abutted, and in which can be seen part of a large archway (21), now blocked, above the entrance to the passage from which the visitor has just emerged. This probably formed a gateway leading to an out-work on the shore of the cove to the east of the castle. A little further north a smaller doorway now leads to a Venetian gun-chamber (22). Originally it probably gave access to the fighting gallery which ran outside the buildings of the Frankish east range. Nearby the remains have been excavated of another length of the earliest south wall with a horseshoe tower containing a cistern (23). The dressed masonry and the thickness of this section of wall make it quite distinct from the sections of the original Byzantine castle already noticed. Unless this and the horseshoe tower survive from some earlier fortifications, they must belong to some repair of intermediate Byzantine date. South-east of the horseshoe tower, in the angle of the present courtyard, is another cistern (24), once covered with a masonary vault, which though doubtless later is probably also pre-Frankish.

In the preserved part of the Frankish *East Range* two large vaulted cisterns occupy the basement level of the first four bays from the South. The next storey, at the level of the courtyard, was separated by wooden floors from the vaulted main chambers above, which were reached originally from a gallery along the facade of the building towards the courtyard. These lofty rooms are the main surviving domestic quarters, distinct from and unconnected with the fighting gallery (25), which ran outside them but which is now filled with Venetian masonry.

It is evident that the east range formerly joined with a series of similar but smaller chambers along the north wall (26), which the modern prison cells have replaced. From the easternmost of the lower cells the *North-East Tower* (27) is now entered. The main section of this is of horseshoe form and projects obliquely from the angle of the castle, but at all levels two symmetrical wings extend for a short distance along the adjoining walls. In the lower chamber, which has loop-holes of simple V—form, these lateral extensions of the tower communicated with the north and south fighting galleries. The latter exists but is filled with Venetian masonry (25); the former has been replaced by the cells.

The upper chamber of this tower is reached by returning to the north-east corner of the courtyard, where a modern wooden stair (28) climbs to it through the only upper room of the east range that now has a floor (restored) (29). The upper chamber is of the same form as that below, but its loop-holes open from arched recesses. The only access to it originally was by a staircase (restored in timber) leading down to it from the terrace roof over the adjoining east range chamber with the restored floor (29). This underlines once more the isolation of the strictly military sections of the castle from the domestic quarters, which they ringed. From the roof terrace an original stone staircase leads to the roof of the tower, the highest point of the castle. A good view of the artificial reef, which protected the castle from sea attack, is gained from this vantage point.

Passing to the roof of the *North Range*, the Frankish battlements should be noted, for at this point the curtain wall stands to its full height, despite the destruction of all within it when the modern cells were built. This wall has three rows of loop-holes, the two lower ones hidden on the inside by the adjoining cells. The height of this wall was evidently increased on two occasions and these high battlements may well post-date the Genoese siege, when engines mounted high on the attacking ships were used. Noteworthy are the recesses formed in the merlons, the solid sections of the battlements, to provide the defenders with maximum protection.

Continuing westward a staircase at the junction with the west range is reached. This *North-West Staircase* (30) leads down to a terrace (restored) outside the entrance to the one section of the Frankish north range that has survived intact. This is a long vaulted room standing over an undercroft (31); it has a large window opening to the sea, a feature suggesting that at one time this section of the north range must have been protected by an outer wall. Returning to the staircase and descending to the courtyard level, a postern gate is reached (32), opening onto the shore from a forebuilding outside the line of the main north wall. This postern and the wall in which it opens is of Venetian date; originally the forebuilding extended further east, to the point where a portcullis slot in the main wall and two corbels of a brattice high above it mark the position of the postern in the Frankish period (33). This postern offers a good view of the artificial reef and of the flank of the North-East Tower with its two rows of loop-holes and a sloping glacis round its base. Back in the courtyard, the corbels and a surviving section of the gallery floor that they carried should be noted on the wall of the west range. This gallery, like the whole upper storey of this section, was a fourteenth century addition to one of the earliest Frankish buildings of the castle, a long vaulted undercroft constructed against the Byzantine west wall.

Returning to the first landing of the north-west staircase, and passing through a breach in the north wall, the main section of the forebuilding is reached (34). The section of the main north wall of the castle outside which it stands preserves much of its original Byzantine masonry. Two loop-holes pierce the Frankish north wall of the forebuilding and an opening in the west wall leads into the *Inner North-West Tower* (35). The core of this tower, at least in the lower storey, survives from the first Byzantine fortress and the opening by which the visitor has entered it is a contemporary postern. The passage which connected this tower with the courtyard now leads to a modern staircase, by which the present top of the tower is reached. Here it is clearly seen that the original thin-walled tower of slightly oval form has been filled out externally to a square outline by a series of massive Frankish additions. Their purpose was probably not only to strengthen it, but also to provide a firm foundation on which to increase its height. Standing over the west ward, into which it made a deep intrusion, and commanding the outer gate in its west wall, this tower was perhaps the most prominent part of the medieval castle. It was doubtless reduced to its present height by the Venetians, who suffered no part of the fortress to rise above the height of their new ramparts.

From the present top of this tower a staircase roughly cut into its north wall leads down to the salient enclosing the Byzantine chapel, and to the top of the *Outer North-West Tower* (4) which the Venetians added to it. From this latter there is an excellent view of the harbour. Small to-day, it was even smaller in medieval times, for the isolated tower near the middle marks the end of the original sea wall on the east side. This wall continued right round the beach, which the present quay has replaced, to connect on the west side with the wall that ringed the medieval town. The latter was but little larger than the castle; its extreme west limit is marked by the white-washed church of the Archangel Michael, which stands on the stump of the angle tower.

Turning back, and passing between the inner north-west tower and the great west wall, the Venetian ramps filling the west ward are reached. At this point, where the entrance passage is regained, the tour of the castle has been completed with the exception of the ramparts and their gun-emplacements, to which the ramps lead and which call for no detailed description.

On leaving the castle some external features are worth noting. A staircase behind the Custodian's office leads down to the quay, from which the *West Ditch* (36) is entered, through an arch in the entrance causeway. Here the catle wall is wholly Venetian. The contemporary revetment on the west side of the ditch, partly restored in rough masonry, formed part of the separate defences of the town and harbour.

Rounding the great pointed bastion added on the south-west angle in 1560, the *South Ditch* (37) is entered. Throughout its length the Frankish wall is preserved and one can trace the loop-holes of its long fighting gallery; these the Venetians blocked, save where they enlarged three of them to form gun-ports. The ditch was always dry — there was much skirmishing in it during the Genoese siege — and this arm has no revetment on the outer side, where the castle faced open country.

Passing round the Venetian South-East Tower (20), where the panel high in its wall was once filled by the Lion of St. Mark, the east cove is reached. This with the harbour on the other side formed the castle site into a promontory, readily adaptable for defence. Both were used by shipping, for the artificial reef which closes the east cove is interrupted by a distinct entry; while on its shore, outside the main east wall of the Frankish castle, there are some remains of defences to ensure protected access to it from the castle (39). To the south this outwork was covered by a circular tower of which only the stump remains (38), reinforced by stone column-shafts salvaged from the ruins of earlier buildings. This tower was linked to the Frankish south-east tower, which disappeared in the building of its Venetian successor (20), with a stout curtain wall pierced by a postern gate. The area outside the latter was later formed into a protecting barbican. The outwork was reached from the castle through a large gate (21), which is visible only on the inside since the main wall was refaced by the Venetians at this point.

Further north, outside a large Venetian gun-port (22), is the foundation of another tower which evidently formed the limit of the outwork in this direction, and from which the fighting gallery further north was doubtless entered. The gallery was filled to support the great mass of masonry which was added above it by the Venetians, but its loop-holes are still visible.

No part of the Byzantine castle survives on this eastern side.

A. H. S. M.

PUBLISHED BY THE ANTIQUITIES DEPARTMENT OF THE GOVERNMENT OF THE REPUBLIC OF CYPRUS AND PRINTED BY "ANAGENNISIS" PRESS, NICOSIA.
FIRST EDITION, 1961. 10,000.

THE TOWER OF LONDON QUIZ

1 Who was the first Constable of the Tower? ....

2 What was the original name of the Bloody Tower? ....

3 In which century were certain soldiers known as 'lobsters' because of their armour? ....

4 At which battle was the elephant armour captured? ....

5 Where were people often buried, after they had been executed on Tower Green or Tower Hill? ....

6 We have mixed up the second row of pictures at the top of page 1. See if you can sort them out.

Picture 1 ('Middle Tower') is really ....

Picture 2 ('Restaurant') is really ....

Picture 3 ('Byward Tower') is really ....

Picture 4 ('Bell Tower') is really ....

7 Why is the White Tower called 'White'? ....

8 What were three methods of igniting the gunpowder in a firearm? ....

9 What is the difference between a joust and a tournament? ....

....

10 Who was the last king to spend a night in the Tower? ....

11 Why was the Lion Tower so called? ....

....

12 What is the difference between the state uniform of a Yeoman Warder and a Yeoman of the Guard? ....

....

....

Answer sheets available on application in person to any bookstall within the Tower or by post from:

Department of the Environment (AMHB/P)
25 Savile Row
London W1X 2BT

ACROSS

1 He tried to steal the Crown Jewels (7, 5).
7 Instrument of execution.
8 The White Tower used to be the home of these kings.
10 Her beasts are seen on a vase in the Beauchamp Tower.
12 Surname of the nine-days' queen.
13 A Cornish raven.
14 If you were this, you came to the Tower through a special gate.
15 The Banqueting Hall was — for feasts and celebrations.
17 Sir Walter Raleigh's young son.
18 Of the many executions at the Tower, that of Simon Burley in 1388 was the — — (5, 3).
19 This usually had on it the crest or initials of the owner.
20 One word of a Latin inscription in the Beauchamp Tower.
21 A raven — practically anything.
22 Swords made of iron would do this if they were not regularly cleaned.

DOWN

1 Colonel Hacker wore a buff one.
2 Sir Leonard Skevington was one of them.
3 St John's Chapel is a fine example of this style of architecture.
4 Archbishop who blessed his friend from his window in the Bloody Tower.
5 Christian name of the man who pulled down the royal apartments after the Civil War.
6 These brothers had a bear and a lion as part of their crest.
9 It was never easy to get — to the Tower.
11 Several bombs fell in the Tower during the last one.
12 This part of a suit of armour protected the hand.
13 Now in the Queen Mother's crown.
16 The Earl of Nithsdale escaped by wearing one.
17 Anne Boleyn was Henry VIII's second one.
18 Princess Elizabeth has it round the edge of her cloak in the picture on page 2.
19 We remember him every year for his part in a famous plot to blow up Parliament.

Make a suit of thirteenth-century armour to wear

Materials: Two sheets of 3-sheet card measuring 62cm × 85cm. (Stick kitchen foil to one sheet of card.) 91cm square of cloth. Black ribbon. 106 brass paper fasteners. Glue, Sellotape and modelling knife.

Note: All sections shaded grey in the diagrams are made with foil-covered card. Cover inside of fixed paper fasteners with Sellotape before wearing armour.

Helmet and armour for arms: Measure size of your head and then cut out helmet shapes to fit. Measure length of your arms and then cut out shapes drawn below, and then curve to fit. Tie together on lower edge with ribbon.

Body armour: Measure and cut cloth to fit (ask your mother to help you make this item). Fix all armour plating on inside of cloth with paper fasteners pushed through from the outside. Sew on ribbons, and fix shoulder armour plates in place.

Putting on the Armour

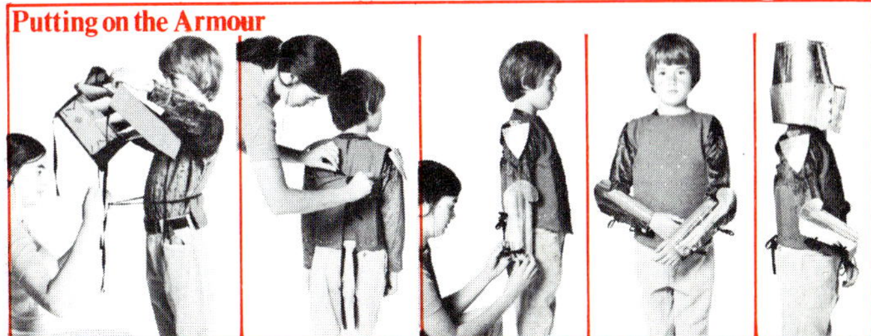

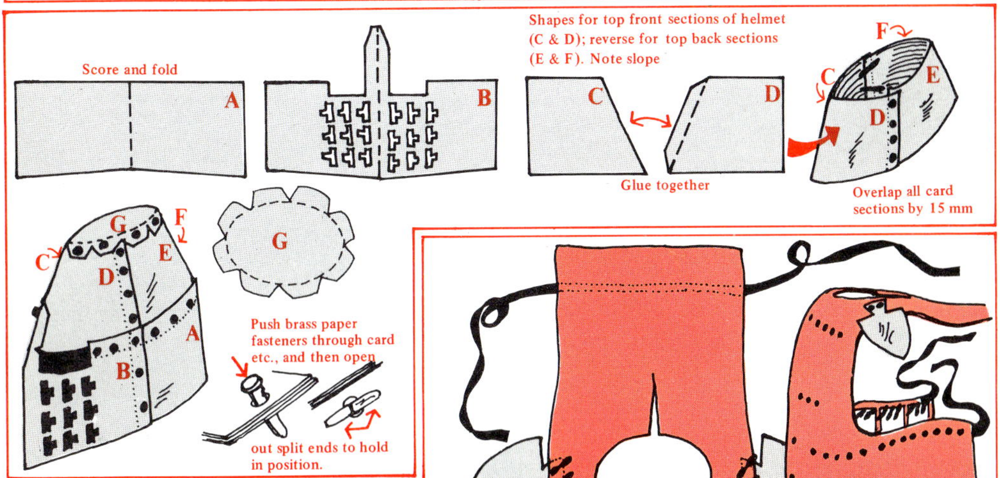

Score and fold

A

B

Shapes for top front sections of helmet (C & D); reverse for top back sections (E & F). Note slope

C

D

Glue together

F

C

E

D

Overlap all card sections by 15 mm

G

F

C

E

D

A

B

G

Push brass paper fasteners through card etc., and then open out split ends to hold in position.

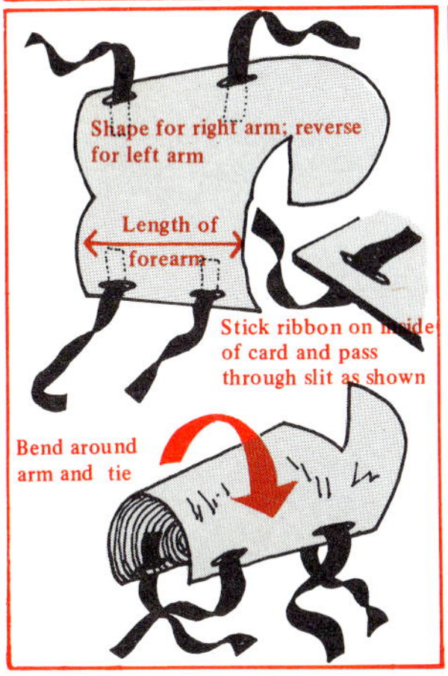

Shape for right arm; reverse for left arm

Length of forearm

Stick ribbon on inside of card and pass through slit as shown

Bend around arm and tie

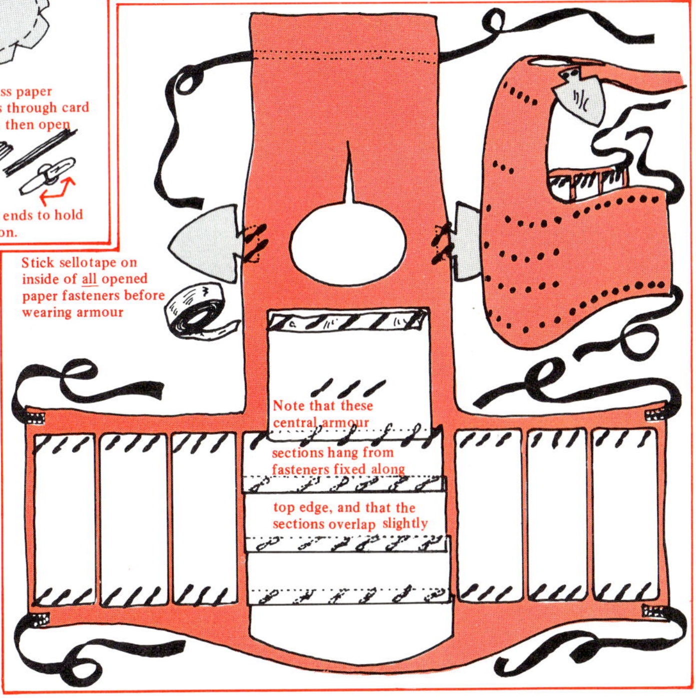

Stick sellotape on inside of all opened paper fasteners before wearing armour

Note that these central armour sections hang from fasteners fixed along top edge, and that the sections overlap slightly

Fifteenth Century

Sixteenth C

his forearm; this is to stop the bowstring hurting his arm when he shoots. The best bows were made of yew. Arrows, carried in the belt, had flights of goose feathers.

Fifteenth Century

By the fifteenth century the knight wore complete plate-armour. His helmet had a movable *visor* over the face. Early cannon were unreliable and their barrels sometimes burst when fired. But they could break down strong walls in a short time. Some soldiers used early handguns, like the one above. When the lever was pressed, the match was pushed into the touch-hole to ignite the gunpowder.

Sixteenth Century

The musketeer wore little or no armour; he needed to be free to handle his weapon. This was the matchlock musket. He charged it with gunpowder from the flask on his hip and inserted a ball from his bullet-bag. The match was soaked in salt-

Seventeenth Century

petre, which made it smoulder slowly. It was clipped into the curved piece of metal (the 'serpentine'). Squeezing the trigger pushed the match onto the gunpowder in the flash-pan. Most soldiers still wore armour and in 1511 Henry VIII set up an armour workshop at Greenwich.

Seventeenth Century

By the middle of the seventeenth century, armour was being worn less and less for fighting. Soldiers of one particular regiment during the Civil War became known as 'lobsters' because of their heavy armour shells like the one shown above. This one carries a sword and a pistol which might be as much as two feet long. He has leather gloves inside the plate gauntlets. Pikemen only wore half-armour, but they were armed with 16ft pikes as well as a sword. With their pikes they formed a line of defence for the unarmoured musketeers.

The History of the European Sword

The first iron sword was made in about 2500 BC, when metal was first discovered. Viking swords, over 3000 years later, were still very simple and it was only in the fourteenth century, when heavy armour appeared, that the sword became a powerful fighting weapon. Distinct civilian and military swords developed and, by the seventeenth century, they were very efficient and extremely ornate.

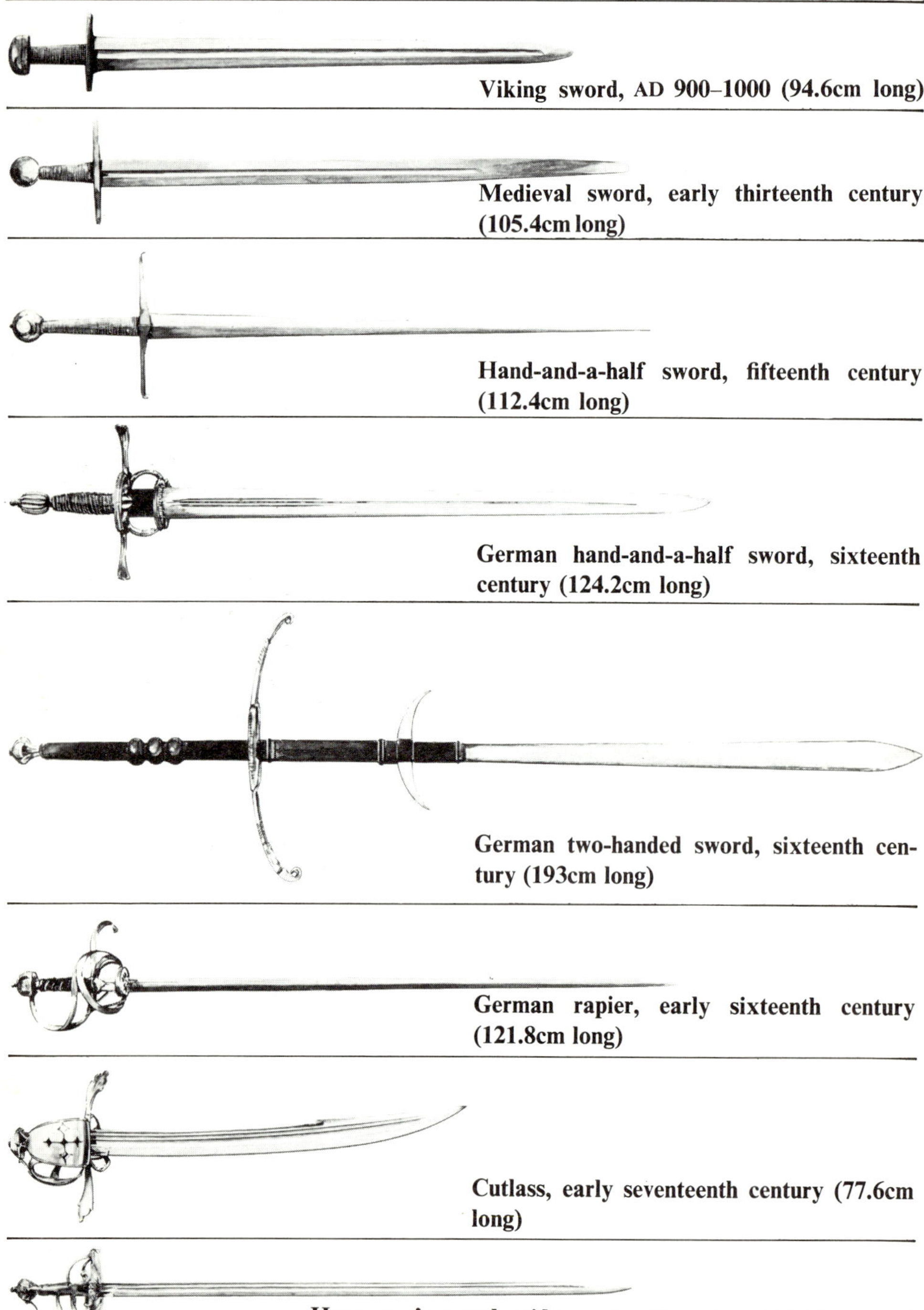

Viking sword, AD 900–1000 (94.6cm long)

Medieval sword, early thirteenth century (105.4cm long)

Hand-and-a-half sword, fifteenth century (112.4cm long)

German hand-and-a-half sword, sixteenth century (124.2cm long)

German two-handed sword, sixteenth century (193cm long)

German rapier, early sixteenth century (121.8cm long)

Cutlass, early seventeenth century (77.6cm long)

Horseman's sword, mid-seventeenth century (105.4cm long)

16th Century Gallery

There are two long-bows in this room, which were recovered from the wreck of the *Mary Rose,* an English warship which sank in 1545. The mud on the sea-bed kept them in good condition, and they are the only ones still in existence. In the same case is one of the earliest types of musket. See if you can find it.

In another case is a commander's baton or stick which has multiplication and division tables on it. The tables helped him to manoeuvre his troops about the field; he could see at a glance just how many men he was moving when he gave his orders.

When you look at the firearms, notice where they were made. The matchlocks and wheel-locks used for fighting and for sport at this time came mostly from Germany.

Most of the armour too was made on the continent, but there is some from England. Look for the English armour. This will show you how all the different pieces could be differently arranged for a battle or a tournament.

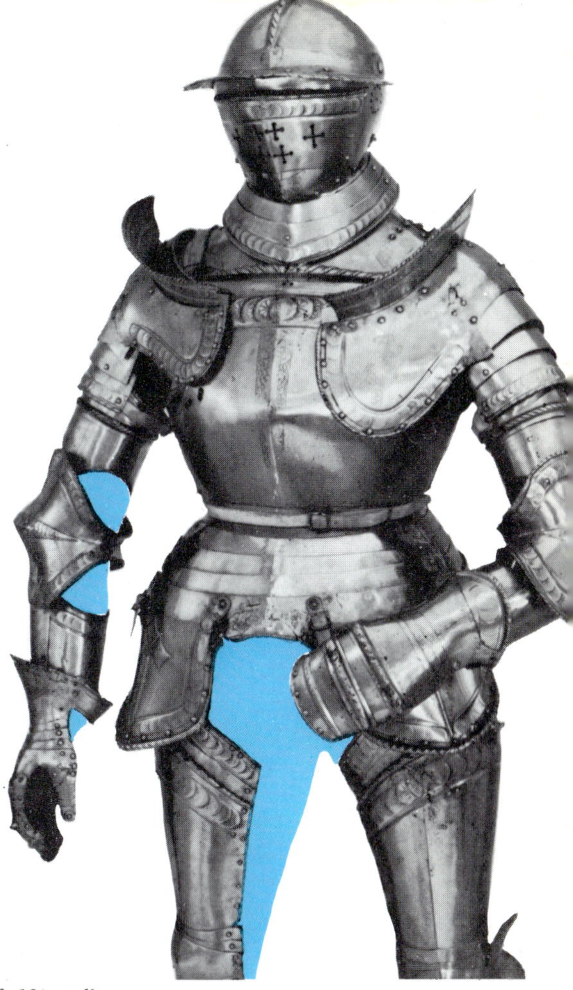

Sixteenth-century armour for a German giant, 6ft 10in tall.

German wheel-lock pistol.

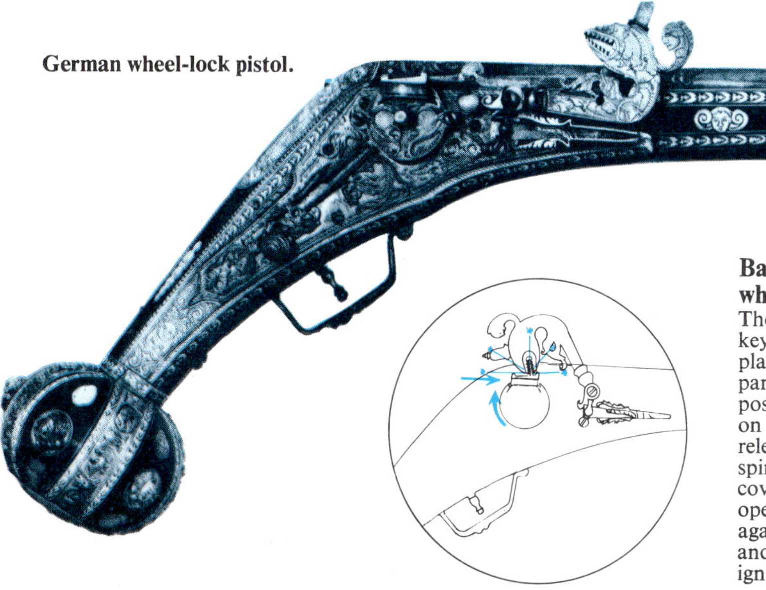

Basic principles of the wheel-lock action

The wheel is wound up with a key and the priming powder placed in the pan. With the pan cover in the closed position, the pyrites is placed on top. When the wheel is released, it does a quarter spin (at the same time the pan cover is automatically pushed open); the iron pyrites rubs against the edge of the wheel and produces sparks which ignite the powder.

The Armour of Henry VIII

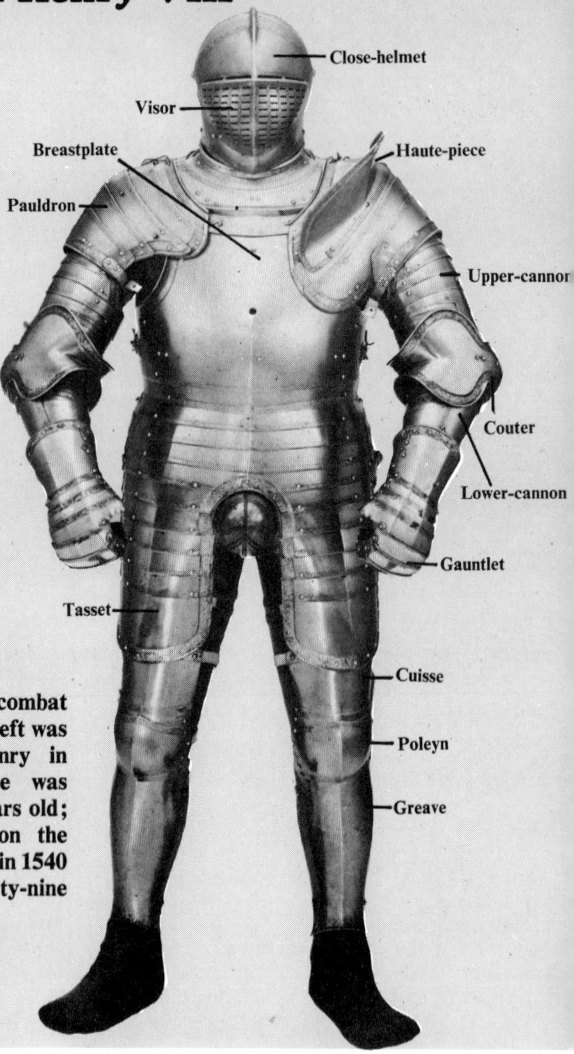

The foot combat armour on the left was made for Henry in 1515 when he was twenty-four years old; and the one on the right was made in 1540 when he was forty-nine years old!

Royal Armour Gallery

The best armour had always come from Italy and Germany, but Henry VIII wanted to have his armour made in England, so he set up the royal workshops at Greenwich. They were started in 1511 and produced some fine armour for Henry himself and for members of his and Queen Elizabeth's court and for the Stuart royal family. The workshops had closed by the Civil War.

Robert Dudley's Greenwich-made armour was beautifully decorated with gold and silver, but much of the decoration has been worn away by constant cleaning.

17th Century Gallery

We have some idea of what famous people looked like from their portraits, but painters had to flatter important people and make them look taller or slimmer or more handsome than they really were. But one way in which we can be sure of the size of Henry VIII and Charles I is to look at their armour, because armour had to fit exactly. You saw how tall Henry VIII was, now you can see how small Charles I really was – only 5ft 2in. Look at the armour which was made for him and his son. The even smaller armour was probably made for Captain Jeffrey Hudson, a dwarf, who was a member of the court of Queen Henrietta Maria, wife of Charles I.

In the showcase opposite is the leather coat, called a 'buff' coat, supposed to have been worn by Colonel Hacker who was in charge of Charles I's execution.

You can see that seventeenth-century guns were very beautifully made and decorated. They were also more powerful, and armour had to be thicker to keep out the bullets. It became so heavy that soldiers began to leave pieces off because they wanted to move with more ease and speed.

Look for the musketeer who didn't wear any armour at all. While he was loading his musket, he was protected by pikemen.

The equipment of a trooper in Cromwell's army.

A musketeer.

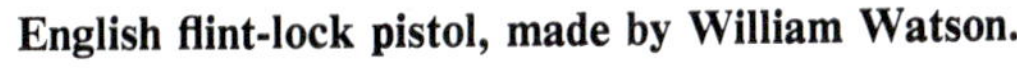

English flint-lock pistol, made by William Watson.

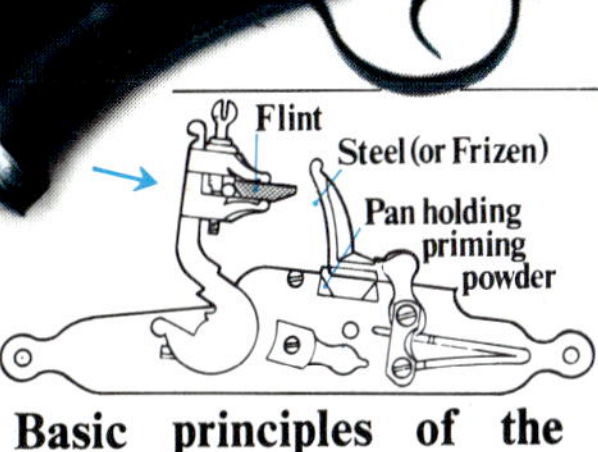

Basic principles of the flint-lock action

1. The 'cock' holding the flint 'hammer' is released

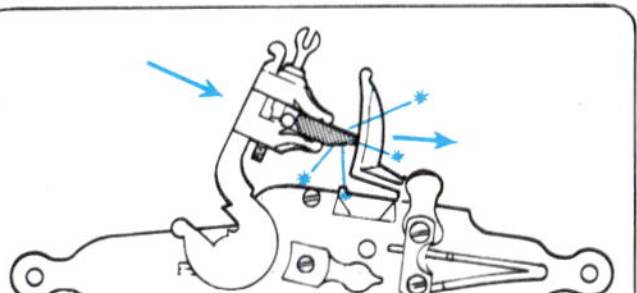

2. The flint strikes against the steel and produces sparks; at the same time it drives the steel forward to expose the priming powder.

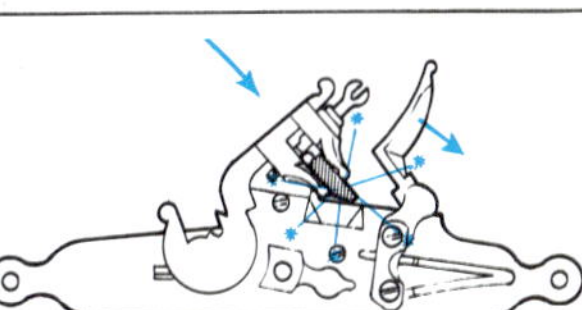

3. The sparks then ignite the priming powder in the pan. The flame from the pan passes through a small hole in the barrel to fire the charge.

Sixteenth-century Flemish falconet.

Sponge

Worm

Rammer

Ladle

Seventeenth-century English bronze mortar.

Seventeenth-century English mortar, capable of firing nine shells at once.

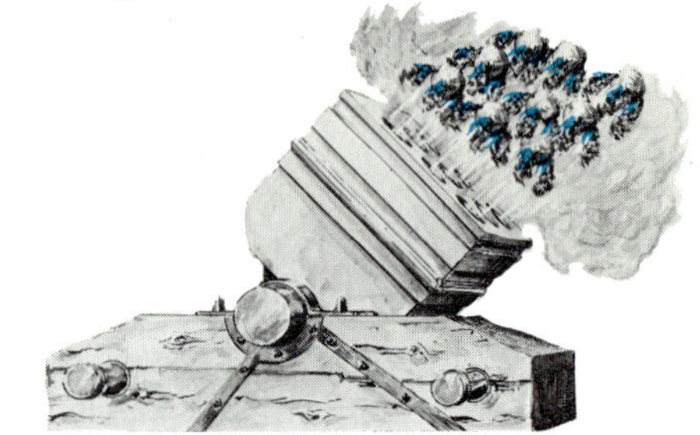

Eighteenth-century English bronze 24-pounder cannon.

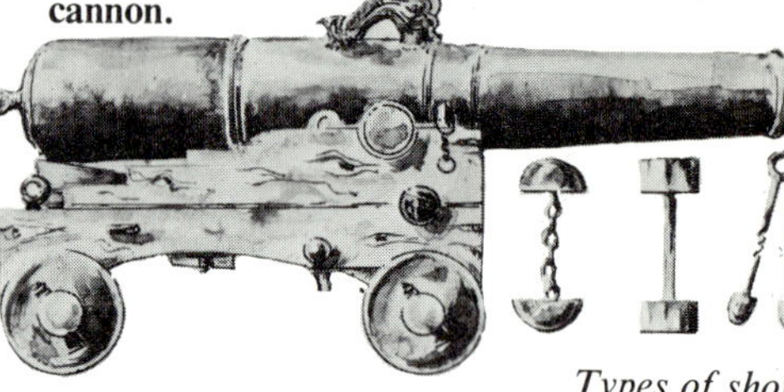

Types of shot

Early nineteenth-century flint-lock swivel firearm.

Buckshot

Early nineteenth-century Dutch bronze swivel gun.

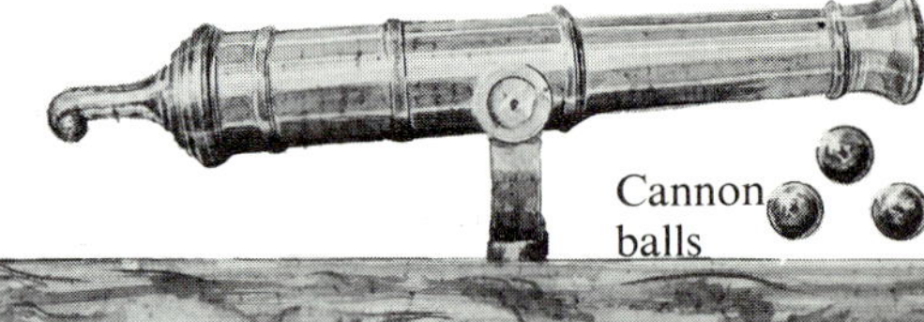

Cannon balls

The Arsenal

The spiral staircase takes you down to the vaults at the bottom of the White Tower. These rooms have been used as storehouses and kitchens. Prisoners were not kept down here, although in the sixteenth century they may have been questioned and tortured in one of these underground rooms.

Father Gerard wrote about his imprisonment in the Tower, where he had been sent by Queen Elizabeth for plotting against her life. He described the torture chamber as being underground and very dark. He was attached by his wrists to a pillar, then the stool on which he stood was pulled away. Despite the pain in his hands and arms, he didn't betray his friends.

There was another priest in the Tower at the same time, and Father Gerard managed to send him letters written in orange juice. With the help of friends outside the two priests escaped from the Lanthorn Tower by sliding down a rope from the outer wall to a boat in the Thames.

The rooms in which Father Gerard was tortured are now filled with weapons from the sixteenth, seventeenth, eighteenth and nineteenth centuries. After the sixteenth century the Tower became a national arsenal, that is a storehouse for arms. Army and navy staff sent orders for their equipment and were supplied from here.

The first room is the *mortar* room. Mortars have a fairly short barrel and fire a shell in the air at a high angle to get over a wall instead of firing through it. You can see the shells of some of the biggest mortars round the sides of the room. These shells have a hole in the top and sometimes a handle on each side. The other big room is called the *cannon* room and you can see that cannon are longer than mortars. They fired further, but not so high in the air, and were used for breaking down walls or attacking troops.

In the little room where you see the great Lion of St Mark there are beautifully decorated cannon. Gun-makers usually marked a gun with the crest or initials of the person for whom they were making it. On this page you can see photo-

The Lion of St Mark.

graphs of some of these crests. Some of them have a crown, which shows that the guns are royal property and that they have been made for the King's army.

See if you can work out which crest belongs to King George II. REX is Latin for King, and the initials G for George and R for Rex and the figure 2 are all there underneath a crown.

One of the crests is from a ship's gun. It was brought up from the wreck of H.M.S. *Royal George*. In 1782, this ship was being careened, which means that the ship had been heeled over to one side so that the barnacles could be scraped off and the bottom of the ship cleaned. The ship leant over too far and sank completely, together with six hundred people who were on board at the time. See if you can find the gun in the cannon room.

Find the guns with these crests.

The Crown Jewels

The Imperial State Crown

St Edward's Crown

The Sovereign's Orb

The Ampulla and Spoon

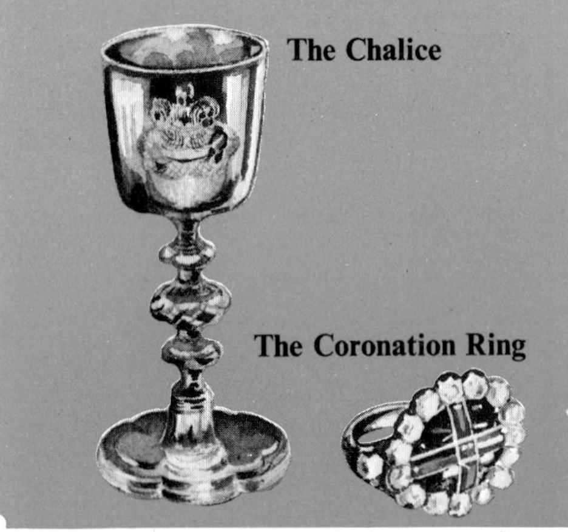

The Chalice

The Coronation Ring

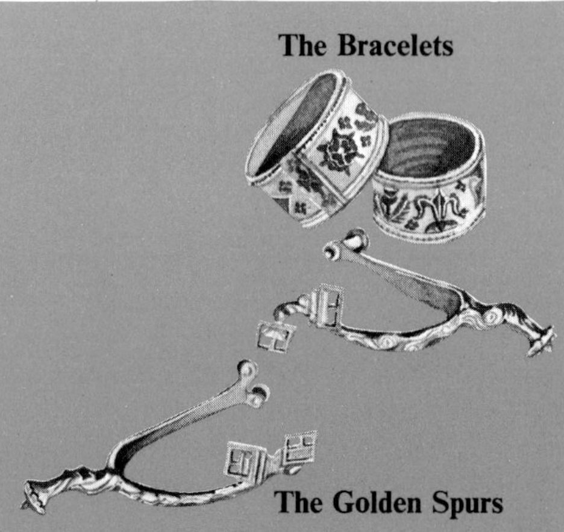

The Bracelets

The Golden Spurs

The Sceptre with Cross

The Black Prince was given an enormous ruby by Pedro the Cruel of Castile as a reward for his support in battle.

Richard III was killed at the Battle of Bosworth in 1485 and his crown was found in a bush. Henry VII claimed it. This crown is not part of the Regalia today.

In 1671, Colonel Blood planned to steal the Jewels. He made friends with the Keeper and arranged to visit the Tower with his nephew.

Returning with three accomplices, Blood attacked the Keeper and took the Jewels. The Keeper's son raised the alarm. Blood was captured and the Jewels saved.

Henry III pawned the Crown Jewels. Kings often had to sell or pawn their personal jewels and the regalia when they were in debt.

During the Civil War in the seventeenth century, Oliver Cromwell is said to have melted down or sold nearly all the jewels.

A diamond cutter fainted with relief after successfully splitting the world's largest diamond to make four "Stars of Africa".

Stamp no. 33

The Koh-i-nor diamond is said to bring bad luck to men and good luck to women. It is in the crown made for Queen Elizabeth the Queen Mother.

Elephant Armour

In the collection of oriental armour there is a magnificent set of armour for an elephant. Clive captured it at the Battle of Plassey. For many centuries elephants had been the main attacking force of Indian armies. Each elephant carried a driver and a man armed with bow and arrow and javelin. The elephants were trained to trample and kill, to move in formation and to respond to orders. When guns began to be used in battle, the elephants became less useful.

General Clive

In the eighteenth century the British East India Company used to trade with India. France had a similar company and the British and French were great rivals.

An Indian prince called the Nabob of Bengal supported the French. He captured the British base of Calcutta, but Robert Clive, the British general, defeated the Nabob at the Battle of Plassey in 1757. He had less than 3,000 soldiers and eight guns. The Nabob had an army of 50,000 men, 53 cannon and elephants carrying soldiers.

Tower Ravens

Ravens eat almost anything and once helped to keep the streets of London clean by eating the scraps of food that people threw out. There are no ravens in the countryside round London, but at least six are kept at the Tower. There is a legend that if the ravens leave, the Tower will fall into ruin.

The ravens have their wings clipped so that they cannot fly away, and the Yeoman Quartermaster feeds them their daily ration of meat. Some of them live a very long life. One lived to the age of forty-four. When a raven dies it is buried at the Tower and another is brought in to take its place.

Even though they are well fed, they love to peck everything and one once pulled the chrome strip off the side of a car parked inside the Tower.

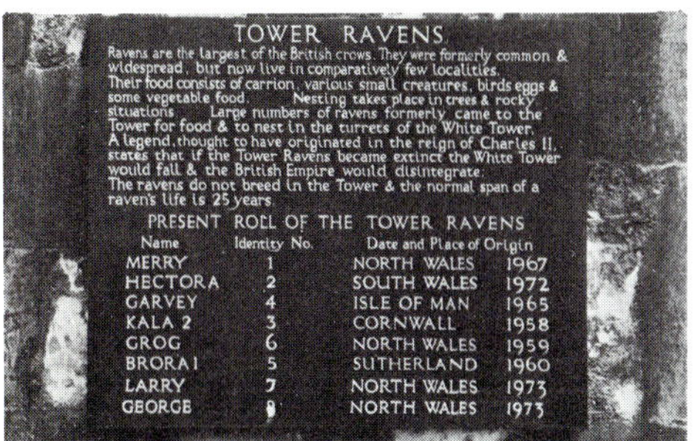

Look for this board.

A Yeoman Warder releases the ravens from their cage in the morning.

Make and fly a 'raven' kite

Materials: Sheet of polythene (0.500 gauge) 91.5cm square. Two pieces of dowel 127cm long. Ball of string or cord. Cloth (leather is even better) 17cm × 40cm. Black and white household gloss paint. Ribbon. Two pieces of paper 91.5cm square.

Construction: On a piece of paper copy out (by drawing up the squares to the size required) the raven drawn below. Cut the polythene to size and put it on top of the drawing. Trace through the raven with the gloss paints. Make the corner-holders and sew them on to the cloth. Then place the lengths of dowel in position (you will have to bend them slightly). Tie the dowels together in the middle, and then attach your lead. You are now ready to fly your 'raven' kite.

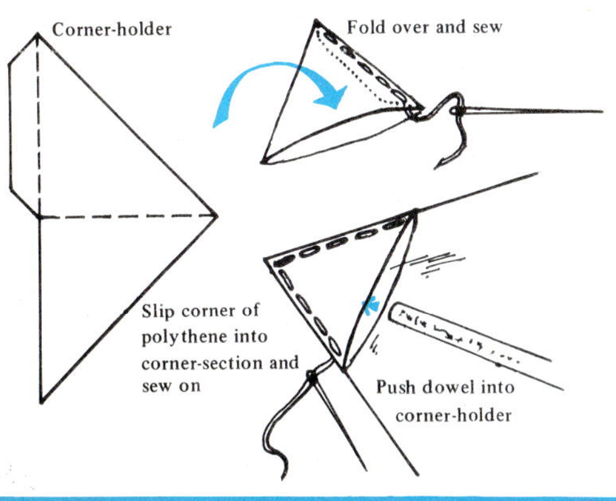

The Ceremonies and

The Yeoman Warders There are nearly forty Yeoman Warders on duty at the Tower. To become a Warder a man must serve as warrant-officer or staff-sergeant in the Army, Royal Marines or RAF, and hold the Long Service and Good Conduct Medals. One Warder is constantly on duty at the Byward Tower; the Chief Warder locks the Tower gates at ten each night in the 'Keys' ceremony. The Warders' scarlet-and-gold state uniform dates from 1552, their blue everyday one from 1858. Don't confuse them with the Yeoman of the Guard: these wear a cross-belt over the left shoulder.

The Honourable Artillery Company Along Tower Wharf stands a collection of historic cannon. Some, captured in battle, have their dates and histories attached. Royal salutes are fired here by the famous Honourable Artillery Company, one of the oldest territorial regiments in the British Army. To fire these salutes the Company brings four guns from their armoury in the City. For a royal birth forty-one blank rounds are fired. The anniversary of the Queen's accession to the throne, on 6 February, is marked by a 62-gun salute.

Uniforms of the Tower

The Constable of the Tower When the Conqueror began building his White Tower he appointed one of his knights, Geoffrey de Mandeville, as Constable. The present Constable is number 152 in a long line of famous men. Until the sixteenth century, holders of the title lived in the Tower itself. A new Constable is installed at a ceremony on Tower Green. He is handed two golden keys by the Lord Chamberlain with these words: 'I have the honour in the Queen's name, and on the Queen's behalf, to hand to you the keys of the Tower of London and to charge you with the custody of the Tower itself.'

The Foot Guards The Tower is still a garrisoned fortress. The guard here is usually mounted by the Household Brigade. One or other of the five regiments of Foot Guards – Grenadier, Coldstream, Scots, Irish and Welsh – sends detachments for 24- or 48-hour guards. Since 1949 it has been the regimental headquarters of the Royal Fusiliers (City of London Regiment). The guard provides the Chief Warder's escort when he locks the Tower each night. Soldiers meet him at Traitors' Gate, present arms while he locks the West Gate, Middle and Byward Towers, and again at the end, when he removes his cap and cries 'God preserve Queen Elizabeth.'

Royal Mint

There were once many mints in England, but that at the Tower was always the most important. The roadway on the west side, between the inner and outer walls, is still called Mint Street. Precious metals were brought here: Devon silver in Edward I's time, Welsh silver later on. African gold gave its name to the guinea in 1663.

Samuel Pepys, the seventeenth-century diarist, wrote of going to the Tower where he 'did see bars of gold melting, which was a fine sight!' He also met Roettier, the famous engraver under whom the Mint was modernised; Roettier replaced the old way of stamping coins with water- or horse-powered mills. In 1696 the old hammered money was called in, and re-cast by the new methods.

In medieval times coins were stamped from discs of metal, with the use of dies and a hammer.

No.................. No.................. No.................. No..................

No.................. No.................. No.................. No..................

Coin Quiz

Read the descriptions of the coins shown above (all of which were 'struck' at the Tower) and then write in the number which you think matches each coin. There are also two stamps to stick in and number in the same way.

1. Elizabeth I: the Queen is shown on a coin called a 'Pound' (diameter 24.5mm).
2. Charles I: the crown piece with the King on horseback also carries the mark of the sun (diameter 46.5mm).
3. Charles II: this halfpenny carries the first known illustration (since Roman coins) of Britannia (diameter 30.5mm).
4. Edward I: this coin shows the long hair, crown and name of the King (diameter 19mm).
5. William the Conqueror: this penny shows the determined head of the King who started building the Tower (diameter 19mm).
6. The Commonwealth: this half-crown piece is called 'breeches money', because the two shields form the shape of a pair of trousers (diameter 35mm).
7. Henry VIII: this coin, showing the famous bearded head of the King, is called a 'Groat' (diameter 25mm).
8. Richard III: the coin showing the ship is called an 'Angel' (diameter 27mm).

Royal Menagerie

The Lion Tower once stood where the Refreshment Rooms are now. It housed the Royal Menagerie. Henry I kept lions there. Henry III was given leopards, a white bear and an elephant by other European Kings. The Sheriffs of London were ordered to provide a chain to keep the bear out of the river, and the Tower blacksmith was paid extra for forging special hinges for the lion-house doors.

The Constable of the Tower was often Keeper of the King's Lions as well. The animal collection grew and in Elizabeth I's time there was a tiger, lynx, wolf and porcupine. James I enjoyed baiting the lions. The last keeper was Alfred Kops, whose charges included a rare 'kanguroo'. Because of its cramped site, the Menagerie moved to Regent's Park in 1834. Long after this move simple country visitors were often swindled by being sold tickets for the 'lion-washing ceremony'.

The Royal Menagerie in the Lion Tower in 1779.

Driving the escaped lioness back into her cage.

TOWER OF  LONDON

Please to Admit the Bearer and Friend,

TO VIEW THE

ANNUAL CEREMONY

OF WASHING THE LIONS,

On WEDNESDAY, APRIL 1st., 1857.

N.B. It is requested that no Gratuity will be given to the Attendants.

*** Visitors admitted only at the White Gate.

No. Percy B. Greville.

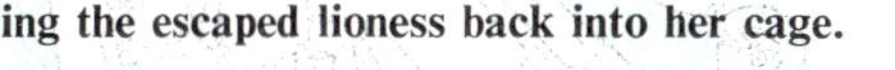

Find an escape route for the lion

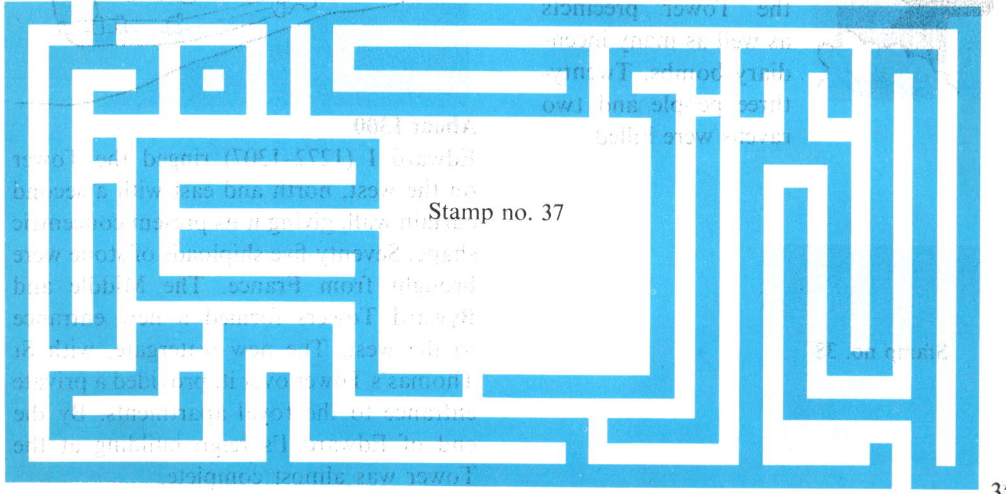

Facts and Figures

It was the custom for Kings and Queens to spend the night before their coronation at the Tower. Charles II, in 1660, was the last sovereign to do so.

The Chapel of St Peter ad Vincula was used by soldiers, Yeoman Warders, prisoners, and occasionally by the sovereign. Most of those executed at the Tower were buried here.

Harrison Ainsworth's famous story *The Tower of London* was written in 1840. It revived public interest in the Tower, which had been neglected and was in need of restoration.

In the Second World War there were fifteen direct bomb-hits within the Tower precincts as well as many incendiary bombs. Twenty-three people and two ravens were killed.

Stamp no. 38

The Building of

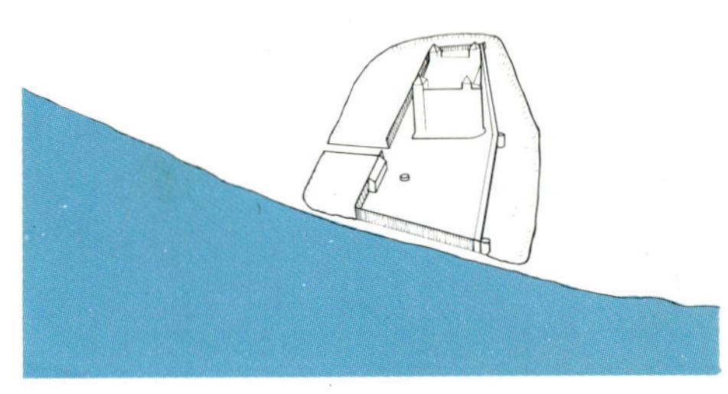

About 1100

William the Conqueror began the White Tower and his son, William Rufus, probably completed it. The Conqueror chose the south-eastern corner of the old Roman city for his castle. Here, at the water's edge, the river protected it from the south and a ditch and a rampart, surmounted by either a palisade or wall, provided defence on the other sides.

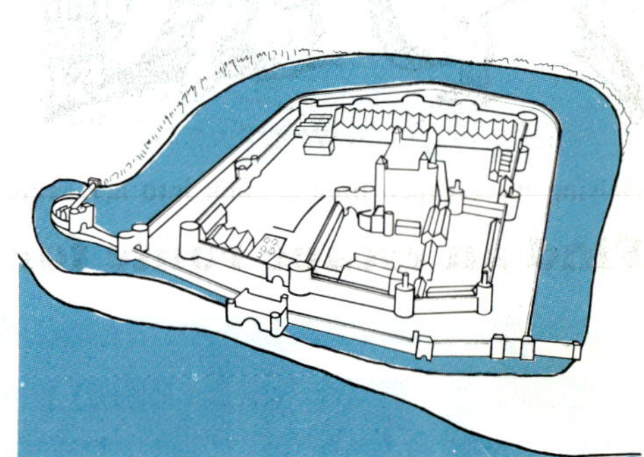

About 1300

Edward I (1272–1307) ringed the Tower on the west, north and east with a second curtain wall, giving it its present concentric shape. Seventy-five shiploads of stone were brought from France. The Middle and Byward Towers formed a new entrance to the west. The new watergate, with St Thomas's Tower over it, provided a private entrance to the royal apartments. By the end of Edward I's reign building at the Tower was almost complete.

the Tower

About 1200
More work was done in the twelfth century. Henry II brought lead from Yorkshire and timber from Kent. Richard I ('Lionheart'), who was often away on Crusades, left the Tower in the care of his Chancellor, William Longchamp, who spent large sums of money on it. In 1190, he had a deep ditch dug all round. He hoped the Thames would flow into it, but there were no sluices to retain the water. The Bell Tower dates from this time too.

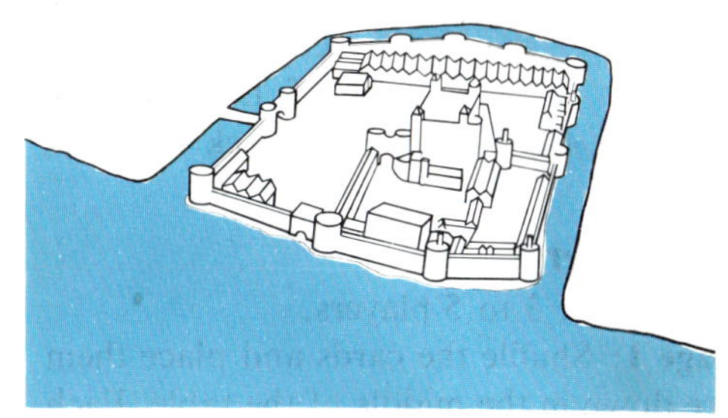

About 1270
Henry III (1216–72) strengthened the defences enormously. He built the greater part of the inner curtain wall, with towers all along it, thus taking in more land to the east. Some citizens were forced to leave their homes to make way for the new fortifications. At this time, the western entrance was on the site of the present Beauchamp Tower. Henry III also constructed a smaller entrance, to the east of the Wakefield Tower.

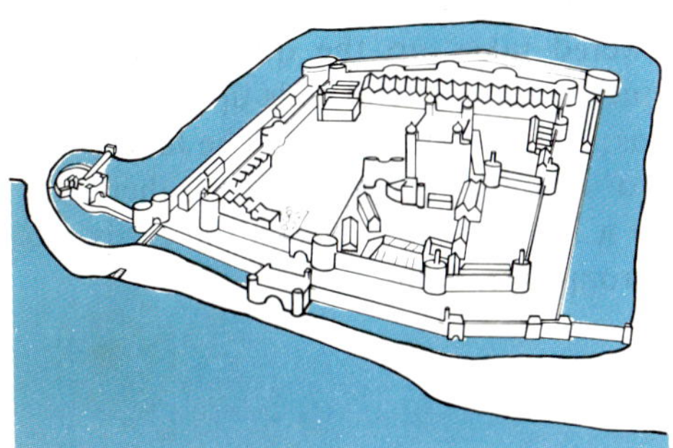

About 1547
Henry VIII (1509–47) added two corner bastions to the outer wall: Legge's Mount and the Brass Mount. During his reign, too, the Lieutenant's Lodging (now called Queen's House) was built at the south-west corner, and the Chapel Royal of St Peter ad Vincula was almost totally rebuilt after a fire in 1512. Prisoners arriving at the Tower by water came through Traitors' Gate, the old watergate. The royal apartments were used less and less.

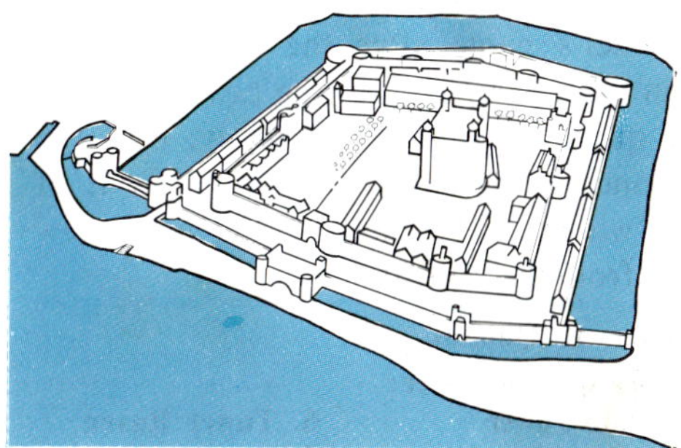

About 1725
After the time of Elizabeth I, the royal apartments fell into disuse. They were pulled down by Oliver Cromwell, after the Civil War, in the mid-seventeenth century. In the reign of William and Mary (1688–94), the New Armouries were built. So was 'The Great Storehouse', which stood on the north side, where the Waterloo Block now stands, and where the Crown Jewels are displayed.

The Prisoners' Friend

A game for 3 to 5 players.

First stick this sheet on to a sheet of cardboard.

One person becomes the Tower Jailer. He shuffles the cards, picks out *five*, studies them without showing them to the other players and then places the cards face down in front of him.

He numbers five pieces of paper 1–5 and puts one on each of the five cards. Thus each prisoner receives a number. The remaining 13 cards are placed face down next to the board, the top card being turned face up and placed next to the pile. This will help you when trying to guess the names of the prisoners.

All the other players should also each have a piece of paper, drawn up into five columns; they should enter the answers to the questions under the relevant numbered columns.

By using suitable tokens and taking turns at throwing the dice, the players travel around the board – beginning at the "start square". After each throw the player asks the Jailer the question printed in the square landed upon: e.g. "Was prisoner No.......... a deposed king?", inserting any number between 1 and 5 for that particular prisoner. All the players then note down the answer given by the Jailer. Each player proceeds in the same way. At the corners of the board a player has the choice of asking one of four different questions.

Around the board there are six "guess squares". Only when a player lands on one of these may he guess the identity of one of the prisoners: e.g. "I think prisoner number 3 is Walter Raleigh." If the player is correct, the Jailer hands over that prisoner, and the "winner" places the card face up in front of him. Whenever a prisoner is successfully released a new card is turned face up from the main pile and placed next to the card already showing.

The winner of the game is the player who frees the most prisoners. However, if after all the players have been around the board 12 times the Jailer still holds more prisoners than any *one* player, then the Jailer is deemed to have won the game.

To play a new game the cards are shuffled, and a new Jailer picks out five new cards.

Start here ↓ *Guess Square*

Was prisoner No. .... a leader of the Jacobite rebellion?

Was prisoner No. .... a Nazi?

Was prisoner No. .... a wife of Henry VIII?

Guess Square

Was prisoner No. .... imprisoned as a princess?

Did prisoner No. .... try to blow up Parliament?

Was prisoner No. .... the last person executed at the Tower?

Was prisoner No. .... a favourite of Queen Elizabeth I?

Guess Square

Was prisoner No. .... known as "the nine days' queen"?

Was prisoner No. .... a good friend of King Richard II?

Was prisoner No. .... imprisoned for his religious beliefs?

Was prisoner No. .... known as an infamous judge?

Was prisoner No. .... one of Henry VIII's ministers?

Guess Square

Was prisoner No. .... jailed as a traitor in the 20th century?

Was prisoner No. .... imprisoned in the Tower twice?

Was prisoner No. .... forced to give up his throne?

Guess Square

Was prisoner No. .... captured at the battle of Agincourt?

Is prisoner No. .... said to have been murdered while praying?

Did prisoner No. .... die while trying to escape from the Tower?

Mystery still surrounds the death of prisoners No. ....?

Guess Square

Was prisoner No. .... imprisoned for life in Germany?

Was prisoner No. .... the last native Prince of Wales?

Was prisoner No. .... beheaded wit[h] a sword?

Did prisoner No. .... write many poems while a prisoner?

Is prisoner No. .... known as a famous diarist?